Good Housekeeping
Consumer Guide

Making Money at Home

Good Housekeeping
Consumer Guide

Making Money at Home

PATRICIA SCHOFIELD

EBURY PRESS · LONDON

First published in 1996

1 3 5 7 9 10 8 6 4 2

First published in the United Kingdom in 1996 by
Ebury Press · Random House · 20 Vauxhall Bridge Road · London SW1V 2SA

Random House Australia (Pty) Limited
20 Alfred Street · Milsons Point · Sydney · New South Wales 2061 · Australia

Random House New Zealand Limited
18 Poland Road · Glenfield
Auckland 10 · New Zealand

Random House South Africa (Pty) Limited
PO Box 337 · Bergvlei · South Africa

Random House UK Limited Reg. No. 954009

A CIP catalogue record for this book is available from the British Library.

Editor: Melanie Sensicle
Design: Martin Lovelock

ISBN: 0 09 181306 9

Printed and bound in Great Britain by Mackays of Chatham plc, Kent

Contents

CHAPTER 1

Getting Started

'You can't really separate the inventor and the businessman. The idea of the lone inventor sitting in an attic somewhere is pretty improbable. By its very nature, invention itself is improbable. If you rush around with all your ideas in a brown paper bag, knocking on doors of big companies, those big companies are going to say no. The way society arranges things makes it very difficult for all inventors. So the way you get around that problem, the way you turn your invention into something, is by being a sort of businessman. You go out there and you start a company and you get your own invention off the ground.'

SIR CLIVE SINCLAIR

Let's be honest from the start, not everybody has what it takes to work from home. Starting a business is more than just working at your chosen occupation, it's the legal, financial and marketing aspects that will take up much of your time. In making a decision to work at home you must first analyse yourself.

Ask yourself the following questions:
- Do I really have what it takes?
- Can I organise myself and my time?
- Can I set clear targets, goals and objectives and stick to them?
- Can I work alone, often in isolation for long hours?
- Am I prepared to, and can I afford to, take risks?
- Can I communicate well with others? You will have to negotiate with suppliers and clients, talk finance with bank managers and accountants
- Am I prepared to work hard to make a go of it?

- Am I an optimist? You mustn't become downhearted even if things start very slowly
- Can I say 'no'?
- Do I know where to go to find information?
- Can I work under pressure to meet deadlines?
- Am I competitive?
- Can I work my way clearly out of a crisis?
- Do I have an accommodating family? Are they prepared to make sacrifices if money is tight?
- Am I prepared to accept failure and uncertainty?
- Is my home suitable? You will need space and easy access. It must be presentable if meeting clients there.

The biggest difference from being employed to becoming self employed is that the buck stops with you, you are responsible. This can be surprisingly difficult to deal with.

You must be prepared to do the parts of the job you enjoy and those you don't – now there is no one to whom you can delegate. If you are used to having a secretary it may come as a shock to have to address your own envelopes and take all your calls.

Be prepared to juggle all the different aspects of your life. Finding the

---

Beware

Beware of con merchants, promising to make you rich overnight.
Nothing is that easy. Always look for the catch and read the small print in adverts. Don't part with cash thinking you'll make money in no time. If you see a company advertising for people to work for them at home **never** send money. They should be paying you. According to the Home Business Association you'd be amazed at the number of adverts around that are asking for £20 or £30 upfront for more information or a starter pack. Sadly, you'd be even more amazed at the number of people, often desperate unemployed people, who reply and receive nothing in return.

right balance between home and work can be difficult.

Don't over stretch yourself financially. Consider whether you can afford to lose money or will failure mean losing your job and your home. Carry out all the necessary research before you commit yourself to borrowing money.

List all the pros and cons of working from home and get your family to do the same.

What kind of work is for you?

Pick a venture that suits your particular talents and personality, taking into account your lifestyle and family. Think about your skills and training and how you can best utilise them. Consider your own strengths and weaknesses. It is important that your new career is something that you want to do and will enjoy. You may have to try out a number of options before you find one that is right – working for yourself can give you this opportunity. It's up to you to make the choices.

A checklist to help you decide

Look at each heading and write down your details:
- Qualifications
- Training – consider even the shortest courses you have taken
- Experience
- Things you are praised for and talents that others have highlighted
- Skills/hobbies
- Enjoyment – can you make money out of your hobbies
- Time – you have this already. You can use your spare time to help those that haven't any, for example setting up a service (laundry, childminding, secretarial, pet-minding etc)
- Facilities – what do you have that you can utilise? A spare-room, large kitchen, empty garage, car, computer, fax, answering machine.

Training

You may need to do a training course to develop a particular skill and most people will need to learn how to run a business successfully. If maths and finance are a weak point, don't be afraid to admit this and don't see it as a disadvantage. You can easily employ someone to do those tasks for you, follow a course or invest in one of the computer programs specifically designed for the financial aspects of running a business.

Most ventures will involve selling at some point. Again, if this is something you are not good at team up with someone who is.

If you want advice when starting up, it's worth subscribing to the home working magazine, *Home Run*. This is packed with ideas and practical advice. A year's subscription costs £72. For addresses and telephone numbers see Chapter 8.

WILL YOUR IDEA WORK?

If your product or service has a unique selling point and is totally original you stand a better chance of success. However, in reality there are very few original ideas, generally people just adapt existing ones – by using new marketing techniques or selling through different outlets and so on.

You will need to test out your ideas through market research. This is absolutely crucial to minimise later problems. There is no point selling perfumes through party plan selling (see page 99, Direct Selling) if there are ten other agents in your area.

Take a look at the market and see what your competitors are up to, the type of customers they attract, location, how they advertise and what their profits are like. You can exploit and learn from their mistakes. Talk to suppliers, mother and children's groups, families and so on to see what they want from specific products or services. Alternatively, is there something they want which is not available?

Developing a business profile

Answer the following questions to help you define your business and decide on a marketing/advertising strategy:

- Who are your customers?
- Are you going to target a specific age or type of person? What is their lifestyle?

- What does your customer want and what will they expect?
- How do you get your product to the customer?
- What price can you afford to charge and what will the customer be prepared to pay?
- How frequently will they buy your product? Just once or every week?
- Is your product a seasonal purchase? How much of your product will the customer buy?

Will my idea make money?

See what competitors are charging. Look at your fixed and variable costs and expected turnover. (See Chapter 2, Money Matters).

In Chapter 7, at the end of each occupation, we have given you an idea of what you can expect to earn. Please use this as a guideline – the key to being successful is to do your research first. In most cases the amount of money you make depends on how much effort you are prepared to put in.

Test market

Once you've done your research it is worth taking time to test the product or service. Contact a representative sample of your target market asking them to answer your questionnaire, either by post or telephone. Alternatively carry out a straw poll. You have to be quite confident to do this successfully because it involves stopping people in the street and asking questions. Stand in the most appropriate place to catch your target customer and keep the questionnaire short. Use open ended questions rather than ones that can be answered by just yes or no.

If you want detailed information hold group discussions in your home.

BUSINESS PLAN

When starting out it is sensible to draw up a business plan (see Chapter 2, Money Matters). This is essential for you to clarify your own and your business objectives. It is also vital if you want to raise money from other sources such as banks. Lenders will want a clear outline of your intentions, project, finances, expected profits and structure.

STARTING UP

Plan to start on a particular day and make sure you work towards that date. Inform your family, friends, suppliers and potential customers of the date so that you have to stick to it. Have a mini opening ceremony, if it's appropriate, even if it only involves your family.

Give yourself plenty of time to get started – allow 6-8 weeks. You will need to organise your office or workshop, order equipment and raw materials, have stationery and advertising literature printed, build up stocks and so on.

Consider if there is a particularly appropriate time to start. Avoid Christmas and bank holidays unless directly applicable.

Keeping yourself motivated (see Chapter 6, Keeping Your Head Above Water). Choosing a field in which you are really interested will help. However, no matter how altruistic we claim to be, the desire to earn money is likely to be your major motivating factor. Learn how to manage your time effectively. It is a skill to be acquired – many of us still haven't grasped it. There are many books and training courses on the subject.

Learn to prioritise your time – list key tasks at the beginning of each day. Colour code them in terms of importance. Use one colour for tasks to be done immediately, another for jobs which will wait until tomorrow and so on.

Cross off tasks as you do them. Set youself goals and deadlines, making sure they are attainable.

Above all, enjoy it.

CHAPTER 2

Money Matters

'A fool and his money are soon parted. What I want to know is
how they got together in the first place.'

CYRIL FLETCHER, British comedian

'First payments is what made us think we were prosperous, and the
other nineteen is what showed us we were broke.'

WILLIAM ROGERS (1879-1935), American actor and humorist

To start up in business requires some capital even if you are working from
home. You will need money to buy equipment and materials, promote
yourself and see yourself through the early days before you get any return
on your investments.

Before asking for outside help think carefully what you need extra
capital for and how much you need. Investigate all avenues of borrowing
and how much they each cost.

First, consider whether family or friends could help, but do not risk, or
expect from others, what you cannot afford to lose.

SOURCES OF FUNDING AND ADVICE

GOVERNMENT (CENTRAL AND LOCAL)

DTI Offers help to assisted areas and regional selective assistance. Also check
out the Department of the Environment's Regional Enterprise Grants.

DTI's Loan Guarantee Scheme This is a scheme for small businesses
who have failed to raise finance through other channels because they lack

a proven business record or have no security. The government provides an 85 per cent guarantee on qualifying loans up to a maximum of £250,000 for established businesses that have been trading for two years. For other businesses the guarantee is 70 per cent on qualifying loans up to a maximum of £100,000. You are required to pay 1.5 per cent interest to the government on variable rate interest loans and 0.5 per cent on fixed loans. If it is a relatively small loan, under £15,000, lenders can grant the application without referring to the DTI's Loan Guarantee Scheme. For full details contact the DTI's Small Firms Division.

For established businesses the DTI's Business Link support network helps small firms identify business problems, produce action plans and access business support services.

Am I eligible for the Loan Guarantee Scheme? You can be a sole trader, partner, franchise or co-operative either trading or about to trade. Activities can include businesses involving goods and services. You must describe in detail what the money will be used for. Application forms are only available from lenders so approach your bank for details. You must present your lender with a clear business plan and financial forecasts. The DTI list quite a few of the eligible activities.

Enterprise Allowance Scheme or Business Start-Up Scheme (BSUS)
This was established to help unemployed people who wanted to set up their own business. You need to submit a suitable Business Plan. Often favoured towards women returning to work and people with disabilities. Apply through TECs which have some discretion at setting level of support and may pay up to £90 per week for 26-66 weeks.

Enterprise Investment Scheme Aims to help small businesses raise equity finance from outside investors by offering tax incentives to the investors. The finance is raised by individuals, who may subscribe up to £100,000 per tax year and receive income tax relief at the lower rate of 20 per cent of the amount loaned. Investment must be for five years. Contact the Inland Revenue or DTI for further details.

Training and Enterprise Councils (TECs)

There are 82 of these designed to provide training, counselling and small business support. Contact your local Job Centre.

Grants

Grants can be a cheap option for raising capital – investigate this area fully. Bear in mind there may be conditions attached to some grants which restrict how the money is spent. Also some grants are repayable. (See also page 93, Crafts.)

Livewire An organisation sponsored by Shell (UK) Ltd, which offers advice and assistance to young entrepreneurs.

The Princes Youth Business Trust The Trust offers grants and low interest loans to people under 30 years of age. It also provides on-going advice, arranges training and offers marketing opportunities to those it supports.

INVESTORS

Venture Capital

This is a means of financing new businesses, developing or expanding existing ones or purchasing companies. The venture capital investor puts up some money, maybe with other backers, to fund the business in exchange for shares in your business.

This form of fund raising is only worth considering at a stage when your business needs to expand outside the home setting. Venture is a medium to long term investment using annually around £1 billion. It is generally for larger sized companies as single investments tend to be over £100,000. This type of finance is more for the ambitious entrepreneur than someone who is prepared just to let their business tick over.

Business angels You can raise sums of less than £100,000 through 'business angels', private individuals who generally commit between

£10,000 and £100,000 of their funds to an investment. Contact the British Venture Capital Association (BVCA) who have publications on how to get into contact with private investors. There are specialist brokers who offer this service.

How do I qualify for venture capital? You need to demonstrate that you have:
• A business with a proven product or service
• A strong market for your product or service
• A good management team
• A solid business plan (See page 11)

REGIONAL SOURCES

Highlands and Islands Development Board Offers grants and loans for industry, tourism, agriculture and fisheries in the area.

Local Enterprise Agencies There are 400 of these throughout the country committed to the economic development of their areas through the provision of help to new and existing small businesses. They are privately owned and funded by a combination of local and national companies, local authorities, Training and Enterprise Councils (TECs) and central government and provide advice and support, particularly on the construction of a business plan. Services vary from LEA to LEA, some may help with training, premises and marketing. They may also be able to advise on likely sources of private finance for your business. The agencies have established Local Investment Networking Company (LINC). This is a kind of dating agency: it can put you in touch with suitable partners or financial backers. Contact your Local Job Centre.

Local Enterprise Development Unit (LEDU) Provides information and advisory services to help small firms in Northern Ireland.

Rural Development Commission This is an advisory body whose aim is to create jobs through supporting and funding established small firms in Rural Development Areas.

It can offer advice on premises, such as turning redundant buildings into profitable developments. Grants may be available for this purpose. The commission can also advise on raising finance and provide loans to small businesses in its Priority Areas (areas suffering from a range of social and economic problems). The minimum loan is normally £5,000 which can be repaid over 20 years.

Scottish Development Agency Offers help, advice and counselling, to small firms in Scotland.

Welsh Development Agency and Development Board for Rural Wales Offers a range of business services including loan and equity finance, a business advisory service, a business start-up scheme.

OTHER SOURCES OF ADVICE

Accountants Can advise you on many aspects of money management as well as prepare accounts, deal with tax returns etc.

Banks It's always worth chatting things through with your bank manager. Most banks offer special packages for small business clients. Although bank loans are an option, remember they will require you to pay interest on the loan.

CBI Confederation of British Industry will offer advice and support to small businesses.

Chambers of Commerce Offer advice to local businesses.

Solicitors A free consultation with a solicitor for at least half an hour may be available through the 'Lawyers for Enterprise Scheme'. Even a short chat may prevent expensive mistakes.

Trade associations and business clubs   Offer useful advice and contacts.

Yellow Pages   For contact numbers.

TRAINING

You may have all the appropriate skills associated with your chosen occupation but you may not have the relevant business experience. A large part of working for yourself is the 'business' side. There are several schemes which may help you to become familiar with this aspect of becoming self-employed. For details contact your Training Agency area office:

- Business Growth Training Programme which offers a range of training options from low-cost seminars to consultancy services
- Employment Training programmes offer benefits to small firms wishing to train young people or adults
- Business Enterprise Programme offers short courses and an open learning package on basic business training.

INCOME TAX AND NATIONAL INSURANCE

Deciding on your employment status

Whether you are employed or self-employed will affect your tax contributions. The Inland Revenue produce a series of leaflets designed to sort out your tax queries. These will help you decide whether you can be classed as self-employed. It may seem obvious but it isn't always that easy to determine. For example, teleworkers may be classed as employees and there are some freelancers, although working for many different people over a year, may not be classed as self-employed. Contact your local Tax Enquiry Centre or Tax Office (see directory for Inland Revenue).

Checklist: employed or self-employed

According to the Inland Revenue if you answer **YES** to any of the following questions you would be classed as employed:

- Can someone tell you at any time what to do or when and how to do it?
- Are you paid by the hour, week, or month? Can you get overtime pay?
- Do you work set hours, or a given number of hours a week or month?
- Do you work at the premises of the person you work for, or at a place he or she decides?

If you answer **YES** to any of the question in the second list you would be classed self-employed.

- Do you have the final say in how the business is run?
- Do you risk your own money in the business?
- Are you responsible for meeting the losses as well as taking the profits?
- Do you provide the main items of equipment needed to do your job and not just the small tools many employees provide for themselves?
- Are you free to hire other people on your own terms to do the work you have taken on? Do you pay them out of your own pocket?
- Do you have to correct unsatisfactory work in your own time and at your own expense?

Complications may arise if you provide a service to several different people, for example do you work as an employee for each of them or as a self-employed person. Another circumstance could be where it is considered that you work part-time as an employee and then run your own business the rest of the time.

If you are self-employed you are responsible for your own tax and National Insurance. Consequently it is your responsibility to inform your Tax Office about all your income. Every year they will send you a Tax Return which must be completed. Similarly you will be sent a bill every 13 weeks for your Class 2 and 4 National Insurance contributions. You can pay your Class 2 payments by direct debit every month but Class 4 payments, because they are related to your profits are paid at the same time as your tax bill.

Being self-employed will also affect your social security and unemployment benefits, and various employment rights such as maternity pay. You are not eligible for the same benefits as when you were employed. You can still claim for sickness benefit which will be based on your recent earnings – you will need to show accounts. You can only claim while you are ill – obtain a Self Certification form SC1 from your local Social Security Office. After a week you can only continue to claim if you have a doctor's certificate.

PAYE (Pay as you earn)

If you expand and take on staff, you are responsible for deducting PAYE and National Insurance from their wages. You are also responsible for payment of both employer's and employee's contributions. Obtain leaflet IR53 from the Inland Revenue for details. They can supply you with the 'New Employer's Starter Pack' which explains most things you'll need to know, such as Sick and Maternity Pay.

Where do I start?

Before you begin working from home you must tell your local Tax Office. If you have given up full-time employment send your P45 to the Tax Office. It will be given to you by your previous employer. Similarly, inform your Social Security Office to arrange National Insurance contributions. You'll need to do this even if you are working for an employer and partly for yourself.

As soon as you become self-employed keep complete and up-to-date records and accounts of all your business transactions. Record keeping is easier if you have a separate bank account for your business transactions. If your business takings before expenses are not more than £15,000 per year then you do not need to send full detailed accounts to your Tax Office, just a summary of takings, total purchases and expenses, and your profits. From April 1997 a new system of self-assessment will come into operation. Call into your local Tax Office for details.

If your turnover is more than £45,000 you must be registered for Value Added Tax (VAT) (see page 23).

On what date do I pay my tax?

This is really up to you. Keep it simple by making up your accounts to the end of the first year in business and every following anniversary of this date. When you have chosen a date stick to it and make up your accounts every twelve months.

Preparing your accounts

Depending on the size of your business you may prefer to use an accountant to prepare your accounts. However, whoever does them, they need to satisfy the Tax Office that the figures given are a true representation of your accounts. Leaflet IR104 *Simple Tax Accounts* from your Tax Office will give you more details.

For businesses with a turnover above £15,000 present your accounts in two parts:

- **Profit and Loss account** – this is a summary of the year's trading transactions
- **The Balance Sheet** – this shows the 'assets' and the 'liabilities' of the business.

According to the Inland Revenue at the end of each accounting period you must list:

- all income
- expenditure – rent, rates, lighting, heating, insurance, repairs to premises, repairs to fixtures and fittings, motor vehicle running costs, purchases of goods for resale, wages and salaries, employer's share of NI contributions, stationery, postage, telephone etc.
- private income injected into the business – showing source and amount
- any cash taken from the business for your own or your family's use
- the amount of any cheques drawn on the business account for private purposes
- the market value of goods taken from the business for family use
- amounts owed to you by customers
- amounts owed to you by suppliers.

This list demonstrates the importance of keeping a record of all transactions and receipts. As well as financial assets you will have to have a stock take which will include all your raw materials and finished items not yet sold.

How do I calculate taxable profits?

You are allowed certain concessions, for example revenue expenditure – day to day running costs such as wages, rent, rates, fuel, motor costs – may be deducted if it is used exclusively for business purposes. If you keep a car keep a record of your business mileage separate from private use. If you incur any expenditure which is partly for business and partly for private use you can only claim for the business part.

You cannot deduct

- capital expenditure, which is capital used to buy or alter assets such as expansion of premises, new equipment
- your own wages
- food
- medical treatment
- clothing (except uniform)
- insurance
- income tax and NI contributions
- council tax.

You are required by law to make a true return on your income every year. Your business accounts should be sent with your tax return or before it if your accounting date is some time before the return is due. If you fail to do this or the Tax Office do not feel that you have given a fair representation then they will make an estimate of your profits.

When you start out it is probably a good idea to put aside money every month to cover your tax bill.

Can I appeal against tax assessments?

If you disagree with your tax assessment you should appeal against it. However, you must do this within 30 days of receiving the assessment.

Don't just appeal if it is too high – if it is too low you will be held liable at a later date. Most disputes are settled between yourselves and the Tax Office. On rare occasions the case will be referred to the Appeal of Commissioners who are independent tribunals.

VAT

Most business transactions which occur in the UK are subject to VAT (Value Added Tax). These transactions can include activities such as rental and hire of goods; sales of new and used goods (including hire purchase); services provided for payment; facilities provided by clubs etc. They are called taxable supplies. If they are not liable they are called exempt supplies.

Should I register to pay VAT?

If you make only zero-rated supplies you may not need to register for VAT:

Supplies which are zero-rated for VAT

- most food (except eating out or take-away food and drink)
- books and newspapers
- young children's clothing and footwear
- export of goods
- dispensing of prescriptions and the supply of many aids for handicapped persons.

Transactions which are VAT exempt

- insurance
- betting, gaming and lotteries
- provision of credit
- certain education and training
- services of doctors, dentists, opticians (but not practitioners like osteopaths)

If the value of your taxable supplies exceeds, or is expected to exceed, certain limits, currently £45,000 over the previous 12 months excluding the value of exempt supplies, then you must register for VAT. The supplies are your outputs and the tax is called your output tax.

As soon as you are registered for VAT you must charge it on all your taxable supplies at the standard rate of 17.5 per cent (some items and services are zero-rated see box on page 23). The person is VAT registered rather than the business. However, a 'person' can mean a sole owner, a partnership, a limited company, a club or association, or a charity.

If your customers are registered for VAT and the supplies are for the purpose of their businesses, the supplies are termed their inputs and the tax you charge them is called their input tax. Every so often if your output tax is higher than your input tax you will be expected to pay the difference to Customs and Excise. If your input tax is greater Customs and Excise will have to pay you the difference.

If your taxable supplies are all or mainly zero-rated you could apply for exemption by filling in form VAT 1. Remember if you are granted exemption you will not be able to reclaim the VAT you pay on purchases of goods or services for your business.

How do I register?

Obtain leaflet VAT 1 from your Tax Office. If you are a partnership you will also need Form VAT 2. Once checked by the VAT office you will be sent advice of registration and you will be given a registration number which shows your date of registration. Expect to be visited by a VAT officer within three years of being registered.

THE BUSINESS PLAN

Even if you are not approaching a backer for finance it's worth setting out and formulating a business plan. It will help you decide how you are going to get started and establish your strategy and objectives and how you are going to achieve them.

Make sure your objectives are achievable but don't sell yourself short –

set short-term goals so that you can measure your progress. In preparation for setting out your plan formulate a SWOT analysis – this involves thinking about your strengths, weaknesses, opportunities and threats to your new business.

A SWOT analysis

Each part of the analysis has a purpose:
- **strengths** tell you which areas you could venture into and will give you the most profit or fulfilment
- **weaknesses** tell you which areas need special attention so you can turn them into strengths or you might decide to avoid these altogether
- **opportunities** are areas you need to exploit
- **threats** are areas which need to be monitored, such as expanding competition, rising raw material costs.

What to include in a business plan

There are many books on this subject and many of the organisations mentioned early on in this chapter will help. Here are just a few simple guidelines to follow.

Present your plan in a logical order, keeping it simple and clear. Write it in the third person, have a proper structure with a contents and summary. It should be typed and bound.
- **Summary** This contains the key issues such as the purpose of your business and the reasons why it will succeed. It should include details of how much finance is required, a brief description of the business and projected sales
- **Background to the business** Set out the history and current situation
- **Products** Include a description, legal requirements, research and development, how you make it, where you will get your raw materials, premises, how many you can make, timing. Also include photographs and samples of your work if appropriate
- **Sales and Marketing** Include market research results, potential size, competitors, customer profile, how you are going to advertise yourself, distribution, selling

- **Management and organisation** Are you going it alone or will you have employees, do you need more training?
- **Financial** Include how much the product is going to cost to produce, other outgoings (rent, materials, bills, travel) likely sales and pricing policy, projected profits, how much you will need to borrow
- **Pitfalls/risks**
- **The future** How you see your business developing.

HOW TO COST YOUR PRODUCT

Setting a cost for your product or service is a very difficult process but also one of the most important. You will need to look at the market, see what your competitors are doing, decide if you can afford to undercut them or cut costs in areas they haven't explored? Explore whether production methods be improved to reduce overheads?

However, don't think you should charge less just because you are starting out or working from home. This shows a lack of confidence and professionalism. Charge what you need to cover your costs and make a reasonable profit. The better the product or service the higher the price you can command. Low prices can be indicative of poor quality and shoddy workmanship.

Be clever with your pricing – who hasn't been swayed by a £9.99 price tag over a £10 one. You could always sell different qualities for different target areas.

Are your products seasonal – can you have seasonal pricing? Can you charge different prices for different parts of the country? Those of us unlucky enough to be in Central London suffer from many services costing at least 10 per cent more than in rural areas. Similarly, if your product is unique you can probably charge more.

Costs

You are faced with two types of costs which need to be taken into account when pricing your product or service: fixed overhead costs and variable direct costs.

Fixed Costs These include
- rent and rates
- fuel bills
- insurance
- telephone
- furniture
- equipment costs (including stationery)
- repairs
- advertising costs
- professional services (accountant, solicitor etc)
- bank loan repayment, bank charges and interest

Variable costs These include:
- actual cost of making your product or carrying out your service
- raw materials.

QUOTATIONS AND ESTIMATES

Whenever you are asked to consider a job always give the customer a written quotation. Think through the work involved and raw materials needed very carefully.

If you give an **estimate** this is just an approximate price, should the final price be higher your customer is required to pay up as long as it is reasonable. If you give a **quotation** or fixed price this is binding on the parties, even if the job should involve considerably more, or less, work than was originally envisaged.

Always say how long your estimate or quote is valid for to prevent later disputes. Also it is worth adding that if further work is required at a greater cost this will be discussed before commencing.

COLLECTING BUSINESS DEBTS

This can be the unpleasant side of running a business but the truth is profits only come from paid sales. Late payment can eat into your profits and affect your cash flow. Interest payments on loans, suppliers and the electricity bill still have to be paid. The longer a bill remains unpaid the greater the chance it will never be paid.

When taking an order agree payment terms and any credit if allowed. Once agreed these are part of the contract. The customer who decides to pay late is in breach of contract.

Have the right attitude, discuss payments professionally and decide how you are going to cope with debt situations beforehand. Do not be over-tolerant for a fear of upsetting your customer. Phone major accounts in advance of due dates to make sure they are being processed. Send a letter to your small accounts.

Most customers will pay up on time, others you may have to threaten to get payment.

Once an invoice and a reminder have been ignored take the following steps to get what is due to you
- visit, phone, write or fax to demand payment
- send a statement containing an overdue message
- send a polite reminder in the form of a letter
- 14 days later send a second, firmer letter which should contain the threat – it is the final demand
- carry out your threats.

Bringing in a third party
Making threats is not pleasant but it might be the only way you get payment. However this is going to cost money, so work out your losses against expenditure – it may be cheaper to write it off as a bad debt, in which case try to ensure that the situation doesn't arise again. If you decide to go ahead with collecting the debt there are several ways of doing so:
- solicitors – they use powerful letters in a short space of time, charging a pre-agreed fee
- a firm specialising in debt collection – the Law Society can help
- statutory demands – a seller can obtain a court order for the debts
- court action – you'll need a solicitor for the High court but not for the County court. Fees are higher in the more effective High court.

Before suing, check that there is no other useful means, that the
customer has no means of paying and that there is no known dispute
– if they are fighting another case, the first creditors have first claim
on any money. There may be nothing left when it is your turn.
Leaflets giving advice on using the courts are available free from your
local county court

- collection agents – you probably won't have the resources to stretch to
  these as they charge 5-15 per cent of amounts collected, depending on
  volume. They are more likely to be used by larger businesses
- small claims court – another approach for claims up to a value of
  £3,000. The procedure is relatively simple. Obtain a summons form
  from your local county court and return it with the fees which range
  from £10 to £65. The court sends a summons to the defendant.
  Often this is as far as the proceedings go – the summons may be
  enough to make the debtor pay up.

  Hearings take place before a district judge where both claimant
and debtor are asked to give their sides of the case. Normally a
decision is reached straight away.

  A fast track will be introduced in the coming year for disputes
between £3,000 and £10,000. There will be a fixed cost and a fixed
timetable of six months.

Business debts checklist

- Do you acknowledge orders in writing, emphasising the payment
  terms?
- Do you get proof of delivery or written acceptance when goods are
  delivered or a service supplied?
- Have you clearly informed the customer when payment is required?
- Do you have proper invoices showing all details and reference
  numbers?
- Do you invoice within 24 hours stressing the due date?
- Do you have a clear policy for collecting unpaid debts?

CHAPTER 3

Legal Aspects

'Ignorance of the law excuses no man; not that all men know the law, but because 'tis an excuse every man will plead, and no man can tell how to confute him.'

Table Talk, JOHN SELDEN (1584-1654),
English historian and antiquary

Before you get started it's worth obtaining an information sheet from the DTI – 'Setting up in Business – a guide to regulatory requirements'. This useful leaflet covers all the legal aspects of starting a business including registering the name, tax issues, health and environmental concerns, employees' rights, premises and which businesses require licences.

BUSINESS STATUS

You can be in business in many ways. The four main categories are:

Sole trader

This is the simplest status and means you are a one-man band. You are responsible for any debts you accrue. Contact the Inland Revenue informing them you have become self-employed. If you are trading under a name other than your own eg. 'Smart Smocks' then you must put the owner's name and address on all the stationery and display the name in your office/house if clients visit.

Partnership

This is where more than one person sets up in business together. A formal deed of partnership is advisable but not mandatory but by legalising the partnership you will be protecting yourself should a partner run up debts for which you too will be liable. You must be sure of your partners. Contact your solicitor for advice.

Again the owner's names must be on stationery and displayed at the business premises.

Limited company

This has the advantage of making a distinction between the owner and the company. If your company runs into problems only the business can be called upon to pay debts, not your personal money.

The name of the company and business address must be registered at Companies House) or you can purchase an off-shelf company.

A company must have at least two shareholders, one director and a company secretary who could be a second director. All or part of the company's money will have been contributed by people who are allocated shares in the company.

Documents revealing who is running the company and its financial state must be filed annually with the Companies Registration Office. You should also obtain a Certificate of Incorporation before you start trading as a limited company.

Franchise

This is where you buy into an existing business idea but run the business yourself. You pay the franchiser a fee, the amount varies. Generally there is an initial fee to cover the expenses of setting up the franchisee in his business and this may include training, initial stock, shopfitting and a sum to reflect the existing reputation of the franchiser. Other payments may be paid to the franchiser depending on the services they offer. You also pay a percentage of the turnover. A contract must be made with the franchiser. Seek legal advice. There are currently about 400 franchise companies in this country. Banks seem to be more positive towards lending money to franchisees, sometimes up to two-thirds of the costs.

The British Franchise Association will provide an information pack for £19.50 which includes details and advice on choosing a franchise and which companies operate in this way.

PREMISES

Setting up your business in your home is one of the major attractions, and probably one of the main reasons, that people start out on their own. Imagine, no cost in terms of time or money in getting to work.

However, you do have to consider whether you will need planning permission to work from home. Local authorities have detailed regulations concerning business activity in the area they cover. These are important for preserving the character of the area as well as protecting the environment. If you start to use your home for business purposes you are altering its intended use and must consult the planning department. If the overall character of the property remains essentially the same, that is residential, and the business is unlikely to upset the neighbours, then more often than not you will not need planning permission. However, if many clients will be visiting you in your premises, don't forget that the extra cars and parking activity may be a source of inconvenience to your neighbours.

Special consents may be is required for work affecting:
- listed buildings
- demolition in conservation areas
- protected trees.

Planning permission checklist
- Will your home no longer be used mainly as a private residence?
- If only one room of your home is going to be used for your new business or if it is used for domestic activities as well then you should be all right. However if you expand you will need to recheck this
- Employing people could make you eligible. However one or two people are unlikely to cause too much disruption to the neighbours
- If you are likely to have a constant stream of delivery vans and lorries coming to your home and blocking the road or taking up parking space this may cause annoyance
- Any activities which create a lot of noise, fumes or involve anti-social hours are likely to invite complaints
  External advertising boards larger than $0.3m^2$ require advertising consent.

Neighbours can be surprisingly vindictive if you encroach on their privacy or upset their lifestyle. Remember, if you don't get planning permission and are caught then you will be required to put things right. For example, if you have put up an extension you will have to remove it which is likely to be costly, time consuming and, of course, totally inconvenient. The local authority will serve a notice on you to cease trading and you will have to find new premises – costly again if you have already had all your stationery printed with your home address on it. There have been cases of people being given jail sentences – you have been warned!

However, proceed with some caution. It might be advisable to try the softly, softly approach with a couple of phone calls asking about a hypothetical situation, eg 'What if I decided to build...' Bombarding the authority with detailed plans may make them more cautious and wary.

How do I apply for planning permission?
Start with your hypothetical phone calls. Then approach the planning department of your local authority and obtain an application form. If you already know exactly what you want, and have detailed plans drawn up, opt for a full application. If you are less sure of your ground an outline application will be enough for you to get a rough idea of what the council thinks your chances are of obtaining permission. Of course you will need the detailed plans later but this way you'll save on design costs if the council are unsympathetic to your idea.

In either event you will have to pay a planning application fee.

Your application is then open for public view. It is put on the Planning Register at the local council offices. This is when you hope for the goodwill of your neighbours. It is at this stage they can lodge their objections which is why it really is worth discussing all your plans with them first – it will save on arguments later.

Your application will be considered by the Council. Their acceptance/rejection criteria is based on whether or not they feel it affects and disrupts the local environment. You should receive their decision within eight weeks. If you are refused they must give reasons and you can resubmit your application within twelve months at no extra cost.

Bear in mind that once permission has been granted you may be required to pay business rates for the section of your home that is being used for commercial gains. The ratings authority is automatically notified.

BUILDING REGULATIONS

If your home requires alteration before it can be used as business premises, building regulations are necessary to ensure that buildings and alterations are safe. An inspector will call to check that the work is complying with the building regulations.

When do building regulations apply?
- If you are building an extension (porch or conservatory built at ground level and under 30m^2 is exempt)
- Altering the structure of the house such as adding or removing load bearing walls, converting a loft into rooms, installing an unvented hot water storage system.

If you need to apply for building regulations, you can submit one of two applications: full plans which show all the constructional details or give a Building Notice (except for work where the building is to be put to a designated use such as shop, office, boarding house). Less detailed plans are required if you go down the Building Notice route. Both should be submitted to the Local Authority.

Alternatively, approach an Approved Inspector, who will advise, check plans, issue a plans certificate, inspect the work and so on. You and the inspector should jointly inform the LA on what is termed an Initial Notice. Once accepted by the LA the Approved Inspector is responsible for supervising all building work. This takes the place of the Plans Application and Building Notice procedures. Currently the only Approved Inspector is the National House Building Council (NHBC), Buildmark House, Chiltern Avenue, Amersham, Bucks HP6 5AP (0494 434477). For more detailed information contact the D of E for their booklets 'Building Regulations' and 'Planning Permission. A Guide for Business'.

Other constraints on using your home as business premises

House deeds need checking for restrictive covenants. Deeds are held by your mortgage lender. Examples of what can be regulated by restrictive covenants are:

- renting out a caravan in the grounds of house
- selling liquor
- converting a house into flats or using it for any business purposes.

You can apply to the courts to have these covenants repealed in which case you will need to consult a solicitor and spend some money. Should you decide to take a chance and not check the deeds then anyone who would normally be protected by this clause (your neighbour for example) can apply to the court for an injunction to stop your business from operating.

Check with your mortgage lender. For most of the occupations covered in this book there shouldn't be a problem. Problems will arise if the lender feels your business will damage the house. Another interesting point is that if a large part of your house is being taken over by your business then they could well feel that they have given you a business loan rather than a domestic mortgage. From their point of view they are losing out because interest on a business loan is higher than that on a mortgage.

INSURANCE

Insuring premises and equipment

It is essential that you are properly insured to conduct business in your home. You may well be purchasing some expensive equipment, however, normal household policies often limit cover to a maximum £1000-£1500 for one item. Your insurance company could well take the attitude that because you are working from home more people will be traipsing through it, possibly causing damage and increasing the chance of theft. You can take the alternative view that since you are at home all day there's less chance for the opportunist burglar! But when all is said and done, make sure your home is fully protected. Go for window locks and a good NACCOS (National Approval Council for Security Systems) approved alarm system. Before you install an intruder alarm, check if your policy requires a minimum level of security.

Basic home/office insurance schemes will insure your property and office contents, provide for business interruptions, loss of money and public liability, and employers liability. Premiums start at around £75 a year. Basic schemes can be extended to cover stock, personal accident, legal expenses, products liability and damage to goods in transit. See Chapter 9 for companies that offer home/office insurance.

Insurance against ill health

It might be worth considering taking out insurance to cover you should you fall ill.

Car insurance

If you use your car for business purposes it may alter your premiums. It's all more money but could save you considerable amounts in the long-term if a problem occurs.

Professional Indemnity insurance

You must get this to cover you in case any advice you give turns out to be incorrect or cause financial or legal problems for your customers. Many of the associations mentioned in this book in connection with various occupations offer this. It is wise to shop around for reasonable quotes as they can vary.

Public Liability insurance

This protects you against claims for injury to other people (not employees) or damage to their property.

Product liability insurance

This provides cover if anything you make or sell causes damage as a result of your negligence in its design or manufacture.

Employer's liability insurance

If you expand and start taking on staff you will of course need this type of insurance in case they are injured in your home or fall sick.

THE DATA PROTECTION ACT

If a company holds personal data on computer, then it probably needs to be registered with the Data Protection Registrar, there are few exemptions. When you register you will be required to give information on the type of personal data you hold, why you want it, how you obtain it and to whom it is given. Under the remit of the Act you must make sure all the information is securely kept and regularly checked and updated. You must then follow the eight principles of good information handling practice. Registration costs £75 for three years. To Register call 01625 545740. for further information write to the Office of the Data Protection Registrar (see Chapter 9 for address).

OTHER ACTS

Contact your appropriate trade organisation to see which acts might concern you.

Food Safety and Food Hygiene Acts

If your business is food related (see page 82, Catering) these may be relevant to you.

COPYRIGHT

The law relating to copyright protects anyone who has produced a piece of artwork (eg painting, illustration, photo, cartoon), written work (eg. play, feature, newsletter, song), music, videos, computer programs and so on, for fifty years from the date they were created. You do not need to register your masterpiece with anyone, it automatically becomes your sole property for your use only. Always make sure when you are submitting work that you have all your details on it and that the copyright is yours. Check who has the sole copyright when you are writing or producing artwork for publications.

PATENTS

If you have invented a new process, product or design it is essential to apply for a patent. This proves the idea was yours. The procedure is quite complicated and time consuming so contact the Patent Office and Chartered Institute of Patent Agents for help and advice (see Useful Addresses). One of the requirements is that the invention must be kept secret until an application for a Patent has been filed.

TRADEMARKS

These are names or logos applied to products or services to identify their origin. They can only be used on the owner's products (or by licensing) and should be registered. Again contact the Patent Office and Chartered Institute of Patent Agents.

CHAPTER 4

Marketing Your Product or Service

'Advertising nourishes the consuming power of men. It creates wants for a better standard of living. It sets up before a man the goal of a better home, better clothing, better food for himself and his family. It spurs individual exertion and greater production. It brings together in fertile union those things which otherwise would not have met.'

SIR WINSTON CHURCHILL

The key word in Winston Churchill's powerful statement is 'wants'. What you are doing when marketing your product or services is to satisfy a particular **NEED** or **WANT**. It is your job to make people want your product or service so much that without it they feel totally deprived. In turn this deprivation leads to feelings of discomfort and a desire to relieve this discomfort. These goods then become more desirable because they can satisfy those needs.

ADVERTISING

Advertising can involve any of the following:
- magazine and newspaper
- editorial or direct advertising
- radio and television

- outdoor displays (posters, signs)
- gimmicks (matchboxes, calendars)
- cards (cars, shop windows, hairdressers)
- catalogues and directories
- circulars.

At the end of the day they are all ways of persuading people and conveying a certain message about you and your product or service. And you have to get it just right. Although you are unlikely to be able to afford large-scale advertising it's still worth bearing in mind that the type of advertising chosen is a measure of the seller's size, popularity and success.

Why advertise?

- To raise awareness about your product or service. You have to make your mark because nobody knows you are there. Many small businesses with great potential and ideas fail after several months because the originator underestimates the amount of time, money and effort necessary to build up awareness. It really can be a hard slog and, at times, demoralising
- To promote unusual aspects of your product or service that would not normally be recognised
- To highlight differences between your product and competing products. Try to create a niche area for yourself with something that is totally original. For example, Fiona paints pigs on almost anything: she has a market stall several days a week and does remarkably well selling anything from wooden trays and hearth stones to cards and letter racks – all with pigs on! People will pay a high price for something that is handmade and individual.

MAJOR ADVERTISING DECISIONS

How much have I got to spend? Be realistic, don't be over ambitious but at the same time if you are underfunded you will never generate customers. And ask yourself how your money could be spent effectively.

What message do I want to convey and how should I convey it?
Most people won't remember lots of claims about your product, keep it simple and concentrate on informing buyers of something distinctive about the product. Once you've got their interest you can wax lyrical about its virtues.

What media should I use? (see below for different methods).

How many times a year should I advertise? You need to decide how much exposure you can give to the product – ie how many mail-drops per year.

How do I know if it is working? Obviously for small scale advertisers this can only really be measured by an increase in sales.

CHOOSING A FORM OF ADVERTISING

Door-to-door mail-drops This may sound basic but what better way to reach potential buyers. Be sensible in targeting your area, consider how far people will travel for your services and where the competition is based.

All you need to do is print your message on an A4 or A5 sheet of paper – commonly known as a flyer. Most computers now have desktop publisher packages which will help you to design your own leaflet. If you don't have access to a computer most printers have design facilities for quick, simple jobs. A designer may give more professional results but you need to consider your budget. Ring round local printers for quotations, prices vary tremendously depending on quantity and location. As a rough guide expect to pay around £80 plus VAT for 1,000 A5 printed on coloured paper.

When deciding on what to say in your your leaflet be clear, specific and brief. Tell people what they need to know – what the service is, how and where to obtain it and approximate costs. Include any unique selling points, for example, 'all garments handmade from natural untreated fabrics'.

The next step is to actually get your leaflets distributed. Asking friends and family to help will be the cheapest way but won't enhance your popularity! If you do persuade them add little incentives such as meeting round the pub afterwards or inviting them to dinner. Do make sure they are reliable: leaflets dropped into the nearest litter bin won't get you noticed!

Alternatively your local Thompson directory or Yellow Pages should list companies who will distribute leaflets for you. Shop around for the most competitive prices. They start at £25 plus VAT per 1,000 but this depends on the area and density of housing. Obviously it will be cheaper in built-up areas. Most companies specify 5,000 minimum.

Mailshots Your local paper may insert your leaflets in the paper for a reasonable sum. Prices can be as low as £15 per 1000 plus VAT although often they will state a minimum quantity.

You can also post the leaflets but it is time consuming stuffing and addressing envelopes. Keep up-dated lists on your computer of previous users of your product or service.

Newsletters Keep track of previous users of your service and keep in touch by sending out a newsletter periodically: a useful tool if you have access to a computer but it doesn't need to be a glossy, professional leaflet. Encourage clients to send you snippets of information about themselves or useful facts. Include good pictures if you can, these are the first thing people look at. Humorous accounts or cartoons will help encourage reading and retention. Keep them up to date with extra new products you have or new techniques. Consider including competitions, special discounts or promotions, quizzes, diary of local events, local theatre/cinema reviews, articles by relevant people and case studies.

Placing ads in shop windows Try to match your customer and service or product by targeting retail outlets with related interests or services. For example, if you are offering a pet grooming service then placing ads in pet shops and veterinary surgeries is a good idea. Your local newsagent is an invaluable display medium. Many larger supermarkets have display boards for local services. You just fill in one of their cards and displaying will cost you nothing.

Make your card eye-catching and unique. Above all it has got to look professional.

Why not add a photograph or cartoon sketch.

Placing an ad in a local paper Think up a good slogan or get a professional to do it for you and consider having any photography professionally taken. Discuss your requirements with the advertising department – it is imperative that the ad is positioned in the correct place. Ever wondered why so many cab firms begin with the letter A? Obviously if you are looking in the Yellow Pages you are going to start at A and work your way through until you find one nearby! Don't forget that if you decide to advertise in the newspaper they may also do artwork for you at a very reasonable cost.

Consider taking out a classified ad in the back of a magazine or indeed a newspaper. According to Good Housekeeping classified department this is increasing in popularity and is cost effective.

It may also be worth advertising in local rags such as Parish magazines, local theatre programmes, football programmes etc.

Press release writing

- Use your business stationery. Keep the message clear and simple.
- Always include your name, address, telephone number and the date on each sheet of paper.
- Make the message as interesting and original as possible without sounding gimmicky.
- Keep it short and to the point.
- It is important to get yourself noticed from all the other press releases so stress how new and unique your service or product is.

Tips

- Keep up-to-date lists of your clients, include their name, address and when they used your product or service.
- Use satisfied customers to get positive quotes for use on advertising literature.
- Encourage suggestions from clients for ways you could improve, expand and develop in the future.

Local directories or trade directories Use these either to get a list of clients or to have your details included. Look for copies in your local library to obtain adresses.

You are, of course, going to be positioned with your competition so you must make your entry as effective as possible. Avoid just having a single line with your name and address – go for the largest size ad you can afford. Use bold print so it stands out. Try to add something that fewer people are offering.

Press releases free editorial in newspapers or on local radio is a great way of raising awareness. Often magazine and general interest programmes are crying out for people who have got something interesting to offer. Send out a press release to the appropriate magazines, local papers and radio and TV stations.

Stationery Business cards will give you a more professional image and of course get you remembered. They show that you are serious about what you do. Again they should be eye-catching and can give you a chance to prove your individualism and creativity. All they need to say is your name and what you do. Costs will be from £80 plus VAT per 1000 for the cards and for printing.

Similarly headed paper for business use is more professional. Costs from £80 plus VAT per 1,000 sheets. Once again, computer packages can do this for you even to the extent of adding logos. A logo could be a representation of what you do, eg dressmakers could have a cotton reel in the corner of the letterhead or secretaries a typewriter.

Public speaking If you are offering a service that is slightly out of the ordinary, Shiatsu or reflexology for example, try approaching local groups such as the Women's Institute, professional groups, Rotary club, Young Farmers, and offer to provide a talk at one of their meetings. Groups are frequently looking for original and entertaining speakers. Give demonstrations and perhaps offer a special promotion if people make an appointment to see you at a future date.

CHAPTER 5

The Home Office

'I yield to no one in my admiration for the office as a social centre, but it's no place actually to get any work done.'

KATHARINE WHITEHORN, *Sunday Best*

Your business may not require any of the following but here is a guide in case it does.

YOUR OFFICE

The biggest mistake many people make is that they think they can easily adapt their current household equipment to suit their new business needs. You do need an office if only to get you away from the normal household activities. There is always this temptation to put the washing in the machine or give the furniture a quick flick with the duster.

You do also need a dedicated place for your paperwork, computer, fax and so on. Organisation and planning are the keys to good business management. If you want to finish work tomorrow there's no problem in leaving out paperwork in an office – but left on the dining room table it's unlikely to survive the night! It also looks more professional if clients have to visit you.

Purpose built offices

If you do not have a spare room in your house for an office Homelodge Building Ltd specialises in designing and building out-houses suitable for office purposes. They are prefabricated and can be dismantled if you move. Homelodge is free-standing on concrete pads which is the main preparation site needed. A complete package is available with electricity – lights, power points and heating included. Internal measurements start at 3.6 x 3.6 metres. (See Chapter 8 for address and telephone number).

Designing an office

Plan the space the way it will suit your style of working. To be realistic the office is generally the smallest room in the house (not including the bathroom). You can probably get away with a minimum of about 3 x 2.5 metres. The smaller it is the more ingenious will be the storage space and design. Whether it's upstairs or downstairs is unimportant but think carefully where all your storage is going to be. Don't spend vast amounts of money immediately on your office, let it develop around you and you will find the best layout.

Creating space   Consider opening up fitted wardrobes or knocking down partition walls (check they are not load bearing). Create more space by replacing normal opening doors with sliding doors, screens or folding doors. It may be worth enlarging windows if you need more light – but of course it will reduce wall space and you may need planning permission.

Decor   Keep decorations simple. Plain pale coloured paint on walls and ceiling is more relaxing and conducive to concentration than fussy wallpapers. Opt for matt to minimise reflections

Furniture   You'll need an adjustable chair (swivel if possible), plus a desk and storage. If you have a computer the monitor should be straight ahead and the top level with your eyebrows. Scour second hand shops and office clearance sales for these. Never underestimate how much storage space you'll need – not just for paperwork but for the things related to your business such as fabrics, dried flowers etc. You may also need room for displays, eg if you decorate cakes, make clothes etc.

Layout   Ideally the layout should be based on the L-shape. The bottom of the 'L' should be your desk with the rest of the equipment wrapping around to the right. If you are left handed then the Main structure of the 'L' should be to the right. It is the same principle as designing a kitchen – your most frequently used items should form a working triangle. This will ensure your energies are spent on your work, not moving from one place to the next!

You'll need space near your desk for the most frequently used books, diary and addresses. Make use of spare work space by using cork, card covered boards or soft boards on the walls for addresses, notices, reminders and so on. Don't forget to have an out tray for post and files which need to go elsewhere.

Do you need a meeting area?

Ensure you have sufficient power points for all your equipment – at least five or six.

Lighting Good lighting is absolutely essential – you will be spending a large part of the day in your office. It can also help psychologically in lifting your mood.

Main lighting: the choice is between incandescent lighting or fluorescent. The former is less harsh but not quite as bright, whereas the latter is noisy and less restful because of its flicker. If there is a central pendant style light in the room you will need extra illumination in corners. Wall lighting or good table top lamps will help to reduce shadows. You might also want to reposition the central light to over your working area. A too bright light can also be a problem, make use of dimmer switches to the get the right working level for you. If you work facing a wall consider strip lighting under a shelf above the work area or concealed behind a pelmet.

Maintenance Keep it uncluttered and only full of relevant items.

Other considerations If the office is on the top floor, think about installing an entry-phone at the front door. This way you can vet callers without having to keep running up and down the stairs. If it is on the ground floor fit blinds at the windowns for security.

Bear in mind that a word processor requires an operating space of about 80 cm deep by 1 metre wide.

Good heating and ventilation is another consideration.

EQUIPMENT

Personal computers

Very few businesses will fail to benefit from the convenience, speed and versatility offered by a personal computer. From storing information to time planning, faxes, memos, directories – in fact the right package will almost take the place of a secretary.

It's worth spending as much as you can afford. Make a list of everything you need to do on it – this will give you an idea of the memory capacity you'll need. Consider if the family will use it for other things such as household affairs, homework, games and so on. Good retailers will allow you to try out the equipment in the store. Make sure proper back-up is supplied by the company. Is there a help-line, and is it available 24 hours a day or just during working hours. Can the PC be upgraded – after all new programs are introduced every day. Go for a modem particularly for freelance writing – articles can be transmitted directly into the systems of magazines and newspapers. It also means you can make use of on-line services such as CompuServe (which gives access to the internet), send E-mail, and fax directly from your PC.

HARDWARE

Choosing the right PC   Once you have analysed how a PC is going to benefit your business go to a reputable retailer for advice on what kind of system would suit your purposes. Sufficient power, memory capacity, multimedia functions, extras such as built-in fax/modem as well as access to the internet are all important considerations and the more you want the more money it will cost. Doing some background reading on what is available is also a good idea.

Monitors There is infinite variety in terms of make and size, from 14 inch to 20 inch, from built in screens to those with stereo speakers. Remember, a monitor is measured on the diagonal, just like a TV screen. A reputable retailer should be able to help you choose what suits your purposes and ensure that it will work with your PC.

Printers There are three choices:
Dot matrix the most basic type and the cheapest. Print is formed by small pins that strike the ink ribbon against the paper. They can be mono or colour. Graphics do not have a very high definition and the quality is not that good. Slow and noisy.
Inkjet tiny droplets of ink are fired at the page through nozzles. They are faster and quieter than dot matrix printers and fine for general text.
Laser the best choice for high quality printing in bulk. They use heat and pressure to fuse the toner on to paper. Gives good quality particularly for graphics. Be warned though, running costs can be high.

Software

Most PCs for home use are IBM PC-compatible. You can run any IBM-compatible on these PCs. Apple Macintosh is a separate system and needs different software. Think carefully about how you want to use your PC and then look at the range of software available before you buy. Most PCs come complete with a selection of pre-loaded software included in the price – you just switch on and call up the menu. However, don't base your choice on the complimentary software, it's much more important to get the hardware right.

Windows is probably one of the best known IBM-compatible computer programs. It is used in conjunction with a disk operating system (DOS), which makes the PC more visual and easy to use, you'll find most business software uses Windows. You can open up lots of software at the same time and choose different applications by clicking with the mouse (a hand operated cursor) on various pictograms or icons (eg printer to print). Some Apple Macintosh PCs will also run Windows and DOS, or you can buy specials conversion software.

Faxes

These are invaluable for the transfer of information and messages quickly. They can be used for exchanging contracts, orders or just product literature. Multimedia PCs sometimes include a fax/modem so you can send and receive faxes without having to use a separate machine. Small machines are fine unless you want to send or receive on A3-size paper, or you can choose a fax/phone/answerphone which allows callers to leave a voice message or send a fax.

Telephones/Answerphones

Installing a second telephone line for your business is much more professional and it will be less disruptive for your family. Another advantage is that you will automatically get an entry in Yellow Pages. Costs are around £34 a quarter for a business line and £99 for installation (excluding VAT). Compare the costs of Mercury, cable and BT to get the best options. If you travel regularly, look for an answerphone with a remote control to allow you to retrieve messages via any tone-dialling phone. Tone dialling or touch-tone phones are connected to an electronic exchange and give access to a number of services. A touch-tone phone beeps when you press the numbers.

Consider extra services. Call Waiting is useful because you are alterted to other callers while you are on the phone and can put callers on hold. Call Diversion diverts calls to a selected number – useful if you are away from home. Call Minder is a recorded answering service – callers can leave a contact number. All of these services will cost you more per quarter. Check with BT on 0800 800150 or your alternative phone company.

SURFING THE INTERNET

What you need

A computer; a modem (the link between the computer and the Net via a telephone line; an account with an Internet Service Provider (ISP) that runs big computers that enable customers to use the net; and software to access different sites on the Net. The software is often included in the fee you pay to your ISP. Windows 95 Computer Operating System has its own Net software. You also need a node, this is the name you call yourself on the net.

One of the most accessible and useful tools is its electronic mail function. You can send a message to anyone in the world provided of course they are equipped up to receive them. You do not pay to send messages across the internet but of course you'll pay for the phone call to your local computer service and you may, depending what on-line provider you use, have to pay for each message you send. What is even more impressive is that there seems to be no limit to what you can send – from picture images and artwork to computer programs and layouts. However you may find the reproduction not especially clear.

The internet can be an invaluable information source – you can tap into almost anything from newspapers around the world to your nearest Chinese take-away. It does depend on what on-line system you have but they all give you access to the World Wide Web. This covers absolutely every topic you are likely to want to cover. You can also use it to promote your company by buying space on the Web (a Web site). Companies are in operation who will sell you space on their computers and help you manage that site. It's imperative that you keep it up to date.

A GUIDE TO COMPUTER JARGON

ASCII file – American Standard Code for Information Interchange – a way of transferring information between incompatible systems
Back-up – a copy of your work. Keep taking copies on a separate disk, so you don't lose work if the PC goes wrong
Booting up – getting the computer going – like turning on the ignition of a car
Byte – measurement of storage. One character (letter) = one byte
Crash – when the computer goes wrong
Cursor – shows where you are on the screen

Database – bank of information, such as names and addresses of customers

Disk – stores information, either ready-made software programs or facts you've put in: anything from a letter to a PhD thesis

DOS – disk-operating system – runs the PC

Download – transmitting files from one PC to another, via a phone line or modem

DTP – desktop publishing – a sophisticated software package that is used for designing leaflets and magazines

E-mail – electronic mail – sending messages from one computer to another using phone lines and a modem. But you have to switch your PC on to find out if you have a message

File – a computer document

Formatting – the equivalent on a disk of ruling lines across blank paper so it can be written on. Many disks are now pre-formatted; otherwise you need to format them first

Hardware – the machines you use, eg PC, printer

Icon – illustrations displayed on the screen that give you your options, eg a printer to print

Logging in/on – using a password, which restricts access to the PC

Menu – a list of tasks the computer can perform

Modem – allows you to transmit information from your PC to another PC by phone

Multimedia – a PC that uses all media such as graphics, sound, text and video to convey information

Port – socket at the back of the PC

RAM – random access memory – used to run programs: the more the better

Saving – vital if you're to store information on a PC. Autosave features do this automatically once you've named and saved a file in the first place

Scrolling – moving text up and down the screen

Software – anything you use in the hardware, eg disks, paper

Spreadsheet – sets out tables, ideal for accounts

The Net – also known as the internet and the information superhighway. A reservoir of information on a network of phone lines and satellite systems you can tap into once you've signed up with a 'service provider', which you'll also need for E-mail. The time is charged at the rate of a local phone call

VDU – visual display unit, also called a monitor or screen.

CHAPTER 6

Keeping Your Head Above Water

'There cannot be a crisis next week. My schedule is already full'

HENRY KISSINGER

'The buck stops here'

HARRY S. TRUMAN (1884-1972)

These statements sum up the best and the worst aspects of working for yourself. It may seem the answer to all your prayers – freedom from commuting, no more tyrannical bosses. But it's the other things that you are giving up that may cause you problems. Gone is the security of a pay cheque, regular hours, holiday and sick pay, pension scheme, support from colleagues, supervision, social life and shared decision making. All of a sudden you've changed from being the monkey to becoming the organ grinder. You are in charge, totally accountable – success or failure rests at your feet alone. The problems are yours, the decisions are yours, the debts are yours. On the positive side the success is yours, too.

Freelancers and home-workers consulted for the purpose of this book all cite similar problems. Here are a few.

Loneliness

If you enjoy your own company being isolated may not be a problem but for some it can be very stressful. It is important to set time aside to go into the outside world – schedule in visits to suppliers, clients and evaluate what the competition are up to. Even a trip to the shops or a brief walk will help. Sometimes a short TV or radio break might be the answer.

Build up a network of people who are also working at home. Trade/professional associations will be able to help here. Subscribe to one of the home working magazines such as Home Run who aim to keep home workers in touch. You might even be able to make use of one another in terms of your business.

Distractions

There is bound to be conflict between your professional and domestic demands. Be very careful not to neglect your family or this will create resentment. Give time to them. However, don't fall into the trap that because you are at home you can sort out any domestic problem should it occur – you are not there to let in the plumber or to look after a neighbour's children if they come home from school early. Don't encourage friends to drop in just because they know you are at home.

Give yourself proper working hours and discuss these with the family. Let them know that between certain hours you don't want to be interrupted and noise must be kept low.

Have a designated work area away from the family activities.

If you have to fit children into your routine, make set times when you can play or do homework with them. Don't feel guilty about having child-care or help around the house because you are at home.

Untidy house/flat

The paperwork you generate at work can be overwhelming, not to mention all the post you will receive. It won't be long before it spreads throughout the house, unless of course you are completely organised.

Lack of motivation

You have to be very self-motivated – the television and the fridge are but a few seconds away!

Find out how you work best – some people find it better to get up, get

Motivation tips

- Have a proper work area
- Don't stop to do household chores while you are supposed to be working
- Keep yourself tidy and organised
- Avoid too many personal callers and phone calls
- Keep any TV breaks to a minimum – if you must watch *Neighbours* switch off the TV as soon as its over.
- Have frequent but short breaks if you work at a computer
- Plenty of fresh air will help keep you alert
- Eat properly don't be tempted to miss lunch, alternatively do not spend the day munching endless packets of biscuits
- Take holidays, don't be afraid to take time out
- Don't encourage weekend or evening work unless it will really enhance your business.

washed and dressed and then breakfast before starting work. Others may work more effectively, starting straight away and then having a break and washing and dressing. Some people still put on their suit and tie before starting work! According to Daniel Collins of Fresh Solutions, one man used to kiss his wife goodbye at the front door, walk round to the back of the house and start work in his home office!

Set yourself goals and daily targets which must be achieved.

Procrastination

We all do this at some time and it is generally when we are afraid, facing a difficult, embarrassing or emotionally painful situation, or are likely to upset others. With some it's just plain laziness.

If the problem is a difficult situation, deal with it now – this will reduce the chance of you worrying about it and creating stress. Make adequate preparations and practise dealing with it alone first. Alternatively break the task up and do a bit each day.

Reframe difficult actions, look at them from different perspectives.

Being taken seriously

Your family and friends must learn to accept your new role. This can be as difficult for them as you. Now that you are about the house a lot of the time, they are less sure about the future, have to make sacrifices because there is less money to spend and so on. From the start involve your family – encourage discussion, listen to advice and have regular family meetings. You need their support now more than ever.

You will only be taken seriously if you take yourself seriously. A professional image is vital, quotations written on scrappy bits of paper just isn't good enough. Children answering business phone calls just isn't the right image – invest in a second business line. You will need to spend money to get it right.

Self-doubt if things go wrong

Let's be honest, it would be an absolute miracle if everything always went to plan. It is important that you do not always blame yourself or indeed your client. Look at what went wrong and learn from it for next time. Always be honest with yourself and don't be too defensive about criticism.

How to be taken seriously by the family

- List the pros and cons of working from home and encourage your family to do likewise
- Write out a list of your terms and conditions – when you will be working, who can use the phone when and so on
- Hold regular family meetings to re-assess the situation
- Ask for help if you need it and don't keep problems form them
- Encourage them to help around the house more. Delegate tasks and give them areas of responsibility
- Do more bulk shopping and cooking
- Don't be ashamed of cooking convenience foods – you can't do everything
- Learn to say 'no'.

If problems occur, perhaps you will not meet an important deadline, then let your client know sooner rather than later. Together you may be able to work out a reasonable solution.

If things go wrong think carefully before making important decisions – give yourself time to rationalise the situation. Face it and define the problem – it will not go away. Weigh up your options and choose the least damaging alternative.

Stress

When you work from home you can never escape work and if you don't get on with it you feel guilty that you haven't. This is stress. Remember you are taking on much more responsibility and authority.

Don't take on too much because you are afraid work or orders will dry up later on – if you fail to meet deadlines or orders this will only create more problems.

What is stress? Ever heard of the flight or fight reaction? Well that's how animals respond to any form of threat – we do, too. While your mind is trying to work out how to respond the body goes into overdrive – extra hormones (adrenaline, noradrenaline and cortisol) are produced, your heart pumps faster and blood pressure rises: you breathe quicker, perspiration increases, digestion stops and saliva dries up. As you take physical action these symptoms stop and you return to normal. Sound familiar? It is not a problem if it occurs occasionally but if it happens continuously stress hormones cannot be eliminated quickly enough resulting in headaches and further anxiety. It can course physical and behavioural problems.

Stress in itself is not a problem, in fact it is an essential part of life. The problem is how you react to it. You need to start thinking in a positive way and analyse what causes you stress and understand how to react to it.

Eight ways to beat stress Health experts at Good Housekeeping suggest:

1. Keep a stress diary Note down at what times you felt stress and your physical and psychological reactions to it. Think how you could act or think differently to help you cope more effectively.

2. Breathe properly Slow, diaphragmatic breathing is one of the most effective ways of managing stress. Place both hands on your abdomen and inhale deeply, your abdomen should rise and your ribs expand up and out as your fingers are moved apart. Breathe out slowly through your mouth, your abdomen should fall and your diaphragm relax. Calm yourself by taking deep, slower breaths out. Return to normal breathing and then repeat. The common misconception is that our breathing is too shallow – we breathe from the chest not the abdomen.

3. Learn to relax Okay, so it's easier said than done. It's essential to relax to lower the blood pressure, breathing and metabolic rate. As little as fifteen minutes will help. Try lying on the floor. Let your feet flop outwards and your hands rest by your sides. Close your eyes and sigh – feel the tension draining away. Breathe slowly and release the tension in your toes, feet and legs. Repeat with your fingertips, forearms and upper arms. Let your shoulders drop and release your facial muscles. Keep breathing slowly. After 10-15 minutes, open your eyes, wriggle your fingers and toes and stretch. Bend your knees and roll over to one side before getting up.

4. Relaxing your mind There are various techniques: meditation will induce deep physical relaxation and mental awareness. Sit upright, close your eyes and relax, breathing with your diaphragm. Concentrate your mind on an object, breathing out and in to the count of four, looking at an image such as a candle, flame or flower, or repeating a word or phrase such s 'peace' or 'one' for 15-20 minutes.

Visualisation is when you image a calm, beautiful scene such as the lake district in winter. Imagine all the sounds and smells and every little detail. Repeat phrases such as 'I feel peaceful', 'I am relaxed and content'. Repeat this before any high pressure situation. Yoga and Qi Gong – an ancient Chinese system of exercises in breathing, posture and focusing the mind are also recommended.

5. Exercise regularly This doesn't need to be two hours running or weight training. Gentle walking for about 30 minutes a day is sufficient. Try to increase this to 15-60 minutes of aerobic activity (enough to make you puff) three times a week. This will help eliminate the stress hormones from the bloodstream and stimulate the release of endorphins, opiate hormones that give a feeling of well being.

6. Eat sensibly Nutritionists suggest potassium rich foods such as bananas, tomatoes and kidney beans; and tryptophan, which is converted to serotonin which has a calming effect on the body. This is found in milk, tuna, eggs, chicken and pasta. Vitamins A and D can all help reverse the effects of stress. Avoid stimulants such as those found in coffee, tea, chocolate and coffee. Drink plenty of fruit teas and water.

7. Herbal remedies Cumin is said to fight anxiety, evening primrose oil, a hop pillow to help you sleep, ginseng for extra drive, lemon oil, rosemary to cheer you up or St. John's wort for mild depression.

8. Add aromatherapy oils to your bath or combine them with a massage. One, two or three of the following to help relieve stress symptoms – basil, bergamot, cedarwood, camomile, frankincense, geranium, juniper, lavender, marjoram, melissa, neroli, patchouli, rose, sage sandalwood, ylang-ylang.

CHAPTER 7

What's Your Line?

'The test of a vocation is the love of the drudgery it involves.'

Afterthoughts, LOGAN PEARSALL SMITH (1865–1946)

ACUPUNCTURE

This is an ancient art of healing developed in the East. It is based on the theory that the body's energy, or Qi, flows in channels (meridians) just beneath the skin. If the flow of Qi is disturbed or unbalanced, ill-health can result. Acupuncture aims to restore and maintain this balance by the insertion of needles into specific points just beneath the skin surface. The tongue is also sometimes examined as is the pulse.

It is claimed it can help relieve pain, anxiety, arthritis, eczema, sports injuries, hayfever, asthma, migraine, high blood pressure, menstrual disorders, intestinal problems and pregnancy management and delivery.

During consultation the client's medical history and lifestyle is ascertained because the aim is to treat the 'whole' person not just a specific complaint. Treatment involves inserting needles at the appropriate points and leaving them in place for 20-30 minutes.

Getting started Acupuncture can be practised at home but because needles are involved very strict hygiene procedures must be adhered to.

You must have a room set aside for practising which is not be used for any other purpose. It must be easy to clean and well ventilated.

You will need a treatment couch, washing facilities, autoclave or other approved sterilisation equipment, paper tissues and towels, alcohol-impregnated swabs, disinfectant, disposable pre-sterilised solid needles or reusable ones, dishes, forceps and other appropriate equipment. It is also recommended that you keep up-to-date records of your patients including dates and times of appointments.

You should be registered with the British Acupuncture Council (BAcC) who have strict codes of conduct covering premises and sterilisation of equipment. They are also aiming to have state registration for acupuncturists.

Qualifications There are short weekend courses which you can attend but if you aim to pursue this as a career, to be recognised by the BAcC you will need a minimum of three years (part-time) training. Contact the Council for lists of recommended colleges.

Promoting yourself If you are registered with the Council they send out lists of registered members to possible clients. Also advertise in local directories and Yellow Pages, leaflets, health food shops and chemists.

Potential earnings For initial consultations acupuncturists charge between £30 and £50 depending on location. Follow up treatments cost from £25 to £40.

Useful contacts
British Acupuncture Council (BAcC)
206-208 Latimer Road, London W10 6RE
Tel: 0181-964 0222

ANIMAL BOARDING ESTABLISHMENTS

Luxury accommodation with piped music, private veranda and garden, à la carte menu and room service all for just £3.50 a night. If you can provide this, running a cattery or kennel could be for you!

On a serious note, setting up a boarding home for pets is very hard work and to run it successfully and in the best interests of the pets (not their owners) means you won't make your fortune. It's more of a labour of love.

Getting started First of all you must obtain planning permission from your local authority – this might be difficult if you have neighbours in close proximity. A garden full of barking dogs is not a way to win friends. So the first caution is, unless you have a large area of grass and are well away from other inhabitants, forget it! Catteries may be slightly different as their inmates are quieter.

All boarding establishments must be licenced in accordance with the Animal Boarding Establishments Act 1963. Licences are issued by local authorities and are renewed annually, as long as the inspectors (generally animal wardens or veterinary surgeons) are satisfied with the standards. The Act defines size and construction of accommodation, number of animals allowed according to the size of the establishment, exercise facilities, that the kitchen area must be clean and hygenic, special isolation areas for sick animals, adequate security (fencing and netting to keep them in and others out) and fire safety equipment.

Adequate insurance is essential to cover you for accidental injury or loss. This should cover buildings and veterinary fees for sickness caused as a result of the animal's stay. A devastated pet owner can be relentless and does little for your reputation.

You must keep a register of the animals received at the establishment and include in it the following details:

- date of arrival and departure
- name and address of owners at home and emergency contact number
- name of animal, as well as any other identification mark such as microchip number or tattoo
- description, age, breed and sex of animal
- name and address of animal's veterinary surgeon
- vacination records
- anticipated and actual date of departure
- health, welfare and nutrition requirements.

It's always worth giving the owners a list of questions to answer prior to their pets boarding with you. The questions should cover areas such as special dietary requirements, medical history, exercise routine, to name but a few. The questionnaire will cover you if problems occur and help the animals stay to be as painless as possible.

This kind of work can be restricting as a responsible person must be resident at all times in case of emergency and must visit and inspect the animals at regular intervals. It's hard work, too. All the animals have to be exercised daily, all areas cleaned, food prepared, waste disposed of, animals should be visited at least three times daily.

Qualifications You don't need any formal qualifications but you must have a vast experience of the animals you are boarding. There are short training courses on pet management. Contact one of the professional bodies for details.

Promoting yourself Advertise yourself by putting cards in pet shops, local vets and of course local papers and directories. It's also worth joining The Pet Care Trust, which has a special section for boarding kennels and catteries. They have their own Pet Care Charter to promote animal welfare.

Potential earnings This varies depending on location and the type of client you are going to attract. Fees vary from £3.50 a day for cats and £4.50 for small dogs in rural areas to £10 plus in London. You will have to negotiate with the owner if they are boarding several animals with you.

You may be able to add on extra for heating, baths and grooming, insurance and so on. Food and accessory sales can be a profitable add-on service. After the high inital outlay on construction, day to day costs will include food, feed bowls, cleaning equipment, bedding material, litter etc. As your business grows you will need to take on extra staff.

Useful contacts
Pet Care Trust
Bedford Business Centre, 170 Mile Road, Bedford MK42 9TW
Tel: 01234 273933

The Kennel Club
1 Clarges Street, London W1Y 8AB
Tel: 0171 493 6651

The Animal Boarding Advisory Bureau
c/o Blue Grass Animal Hotel, Clatterwick Lane, Little Leigh
Near Northwich CW8 4RJ
Tel: 01606 891303

The Feline Advisory Bureau
Boarding Cattery Information Service, 1 Church Close, Orcheston, Salisbury,
Wiltshire SP3 4RP
Tel: 01980 621201

Pet Plan Ltd
West Cross House, 2 West Cross Way, Brentford, Middlesex TW8 9DX
Tel: 0181 580 8000

ANTIQUE DEALING

So, you fancy yourself as a budding Lovejoy!

With the proliferation of antiques fairs and markets, antique dealing from home is a real possibility. It has increased in popularity because of TV programmes like the Antiques Roadshow which has really brought it into the public eye.

Just for interest, an antique is defined by the British Antique Dealer's Association (BADA) as, 'an object that was manufactured more than a hundred years prior to the date on which it is offered for sale and which is in substantially the same condition as when originally made and has never been added to or changed in any significant way except when repairs have been essential'.

Getting started You will need some capital to buy your stock and a secure area for storing the antiques. They can be viewed by appointment only or by exhibiting at fairs and markets.

It's worth joining a trade association like BADA which will give you exposure and publicity.

Qualifications You don't need any formal qualifications but what you do need is experience, knowledge, starting capital and the will to work hard. You also need a bit of salesmanship and an eye for spotting a good deal. The greater your starting capital the more chance you have of building up a good stock and selling it on to interested parties. You may have to travel miles to find that essential piece.

You may be able to make 'pocket-money' if you start with limited funding but it will be much harder to build it into a full-time career.

It may be useful to decide if you want to specialise in a particular field or period or you may feel you want a broad overall knowledge.

At one end of the scale you can take a degree or diploma in fine or applied arts or start at the bottom as an antique dealers assistant which is a sort of apprenticeship. Some universities run courses but getting a place is very competitive. You may be better off doing a private course which is shorter and more geared up to antiques in general. These are expensive though, expect to pay about £2,000 for a short course and up to £5,000 for a one year diploma course. Some examples are: Christie's Fine Arts Course; Courtauld Institute of Art; Fine Art Tutors; Inchbald School of Design; Sotheby's; Study Centre for the History of the Fine and Decorative Arts.

Of course there is nothing stopping you from building up your own knowledge through reading the appropriate books, visiting museums and stately homes, going to auctions, dealers showrooms and markets. Try part-time evening courses such as the one run by Birkbeck College or short courses run by West Dean College which you'll find much cheaper.

The BADA and the London and Provincial Antique Dealers Association can help with general information such as details of the major Antique Fairs in Britain and guidance on careers in antiques.

Promoting yourself This will be very much word of mouth, other dealers may pass people on to you especially if you specialise in a certain area. Start slowly. Try a market stall first.

Potential earnings Lots or not much, it depends very much on you and perhaps just a little bit of luck.

Useful contacts

The British Antique Dealers' Association
20 Rutland Gate, London SW7 1BD
Tel: 0171 589 4128

London and Provincial Antique Dealers Association
535 Kings Road, London SW10 0SZ
Tel: 0171 823 3511

Birkbeck College
Malet Street, London WC1E 7HX
Tel: 0171 631 6110

Christie's Education
63 Old Brompton Road, London SW7 3JS
Tel: 0171 581 3933

Courtauld Institute of Art
Somerset House, Strand, London WC2R 0RN
Tel: 0171 872 0220

Fine Art Tutors
85 Belsize Park Gardens, London NW3
Tel: 0171 586 0312

Inchbald School of Design
7 Eaton Gate' London SW1 W9BA
Tel: 0171 730 5508

Sotheby's Institute
30 Oxford Street, London W1N 9FL
Tel: 0171 323 5775

Study Centre for the History of the Fine and Decorative Arts
9 Westwood Gardens, London SW13 0LB
Tel: 0181 876 3773

West Dean College
West Dean, Chichester, West Sussex PO18 0QZ
Tel: 01243 811301

ANTIQUES AND PICTURE RESTORATION

This is a very specialist business and you do need training and qualifications to set yourself up as a restorer. Experience here is invaluable.

It's worth contacting the Conservation Unit of the Museums and Galleries Commission who maintain a register of conservation practices around the UK. The aim of this is to promote and raise standards in conservation. If you wish to be included on their register as an owner or manager you should have at least seven years experience in your specialist field including any period of training. A formal conservation qualification is preferable.

Getting started You can quite easily work from home but it must be in a separate area from your living accommodation and you will need quite a lot of specialist equipment and tools which can be costly. For example you will need extraction for toxic fumes, enclosed areas for varnishing, safety equipment, and good fire escapes. The costs can be several thousands of pounds.

Join one of the professional trade organisations. This shows your clients that you have a commitment to professional standards and ethics. For example

Membership of The British Antique Furniture Restorers' Association(BAFRA), Fellowship of The Association of British Picture Restorers(ABPR) and accreditation by The British Society of Master Glass Painters – BSMGP. The Conservation Group indicates a special level of recognition by these bodies. Fellowship of the International Institute for Conservation(IIC) denotes particular recognition of services to the profession. Contact these associations for details of membership.

The Conservation Unit issues guidelines of good practice which is worth obtaining.

Ensure you have excellent security arrangements – you may have to store some valuable pieces. Check your insurance is adequate and covers transportation to and from your workshop.

You may be working with hazardous chemicals so health and safety issues must be considered. Find out about COSSH regulations.

Qualifications According to the Association of British Picture Restorers (ABPR) you will need 'artistic ability, manual dexterity, good colour vision, some scientific training, patience and great perseverance'. If you wish to train in this area send your details through to the ABPR who will forward your details to Fellows who have vacancies in their studios. They can also identify university training courses. The best training is to work under a good restorer for several years.

Promoting yourself Stick to one or two areas of expertise and advertise these services. People are going to look for conservators who have done pieces of similar work. Antique dealers and galleries may be able to help.

Keep a portfolio of your work – before and after photographs.

Potential earnings This depends on the type of work you are doing and who you are doing it for.

Useful contacts
The British Antique Furniture Restorers' Association
6 Whitehorse Mews, Westminster Bridge Road, London SE1 7QD
Tel: 0171 620 3761

Association of British Picture Restorers
Station Avenue, Kew, Surrey TW9 3QA
Tel: 0181 948 5644

The British Society of Master Glass Painters
6 Queen Square, London WC1N 2AR

STARTING AN AGENCY

Agencies can cover a range of services, from nannies and carers to house
cleaning. Basically an agent is the link between those who have a service or
goods to sell and those who want to buy them.

Getting started Do your research first. Find out the best ways to reach both
buyers and sellers.

Qualifications No formal qualifications just good networking and
organisational skills.

Promoting yourself Advertise yourself using leaflets and cards in shop
windows for your buyers. To gather your sellers advertise in the appropriate
trade magazines and places they are likely to go.

Potential earnings Your start up costs will be relatively low and you should be
able to build up a steady income. Your charges will generally be commission
charges which will depend on your service and location. For example Paula
Thompson who runs a nannying Agency in Blackheath earns a commission of
£280 every time she successfully finds a nanny, however Susan Beale in
Garstang finds she cannot ask more than £200.

Useful contacts
Manufacturers Agents' Association
1 Somer's Road, Reigate, Surrey, RH2 9DU
Tel: 01737 241025

AROMATHERAPY

Aromatherapy is one of the fastest growing areas of complementary medicine in
this country. It uses a huge range of essential oils from plant sources to maintain

or restore the physical and psychological well being of the patient. Massage generally plays a large role in aromatherapy but oils can also be used in many other ways such as in the bath or inhaled, or in creams and lotions.

Aromatherapy is used extensively in almost every aspect of health care from maternity, intensive care, coronary care, rheumatology and rehabilition, care of the elderly, HIV and Aids, to cancer and hospice care. In these instances it is used to relieve pain and helping the patient to sleep without the use of conventional drugs. Home-based treatment will probably be more concerned with stress-related conditions.

Getting started To set up your own practice you will need a private, quiet room, a plinth or couch, towels, washing facilities and your range of essential oils.

During a session you will obtain detailed information on the patients medical history and lifestyle. The appropriate oils are selected and blended and applied by massage.

Qualifications The Aromatherapy Organisations Council (AOC), the governing body for the aromotherapy profession in the UK implemented training standards in 1994. It represents 14 professional associations and 85 training establishments. The cost of training varies from around £1000 to £3200. The Tisserand Institute offers one of the highest qualifications in the UK. Their diploma course can be taken full-time over nine months or part-time at weekends over two years. The course fee is £3232 which can be paid in instalments throughout the course. During the course you will learn about massage techniques, aromatherapy and anatomy, kinesiology, essential oil science, lifestyle management, communication skills and practice management. They also hold career evenings throughout the year which will help you decide, before you embark on a course, if this is for you.

Promoting yourself Local directories, health food shops, chemists and leaflets. The AOC keeps lists of registered members which it sends out to interested clients.

Potential earnings A session generally lasts around 60-90 minutes and charges range from £15–£45.

Useful contacts

Aromatherapy Organisations Council
(send an A5 SAE)
3 Latymer Close, Braybrooke, Market Harborough, Leicester LE16 8LN
Tel: 01858 434242

The Tisserand Institute
65 Church Road, Hove, E.Sussex BN3 2BD
Tel: 01273 206640

ARTIST/CARTOONIST/ILLUSTRATOR

As well as fine art this type of work can include comic and adventure strips,
editorial cartoonist (providing political or social comment), humorist illustrator,
graphic artist, caricaturist, colour cartoonist and illustrator. You can use your
skills to create greetings cards or calendars as well as being published in
magazines or newspapers.

Getting started You need a quiet place to work with good lighting and all the
appropriate materials – canvas, easel, drawing board, paints, paper and so on.

Qualifications You don't need any qualifications or experience. However, if
you are just starting out it is worth following a course of which there are several.
The Association of Illustrators should be able to help you choose. The Morris
College of Journalism runs correspondence courses leading to a Diploma in
Cartooning. The courses take you through the stages of creating, developing
and submitting a cartoon as well as how to advertise yourself and the business
side of things. Course fees are between £250 and £300.

 You don't need to be a skilled artist to succeed but you do need a certain
amount of creativity, flair, enthusiasm and ambition. It might be useful to
specialise in a certain field, sport for example, so you get recognised in certain
areas.

Promoting yourself For fine art, such as painting, contact galleries direct. Find
out the type of paintings they specialise in and you might be able to consider a
one man exhibition. It's worth purchasing a copy of The Arts Review Yearbook
which contains listing of the main galleries. The usual procedure is to write to
the director first, giving a description of the type of work you do together with

some photographs. Consider displaying at the annual Summer Exhibition at the Royal Academy in London which accepts work from anyone. Submissions are presented to the Selection Committee and the Hanging Committee. Obtain details by sending an SAE to The Registry of the Royal Academy, early in February.

More locally you could sell to local art shops or accept commissions for painting portraits or if you live in a tourist area paint people's portraits during the season.

Illustrators should contact the design or editorial departments of publishing houses, first by letter than a follow up call to show your portfolio.

Even companies involved in finance or in the public sector need cartoons and illustrations at some time for in-house magazines or publicity information. Local restaurants or pubs may also want your services for menus or decorations.

Market stalls and fairs are a good way to advertise yourself, particularly if you do personalised gifts such as T-shirts or cards. Contact the major publishing houses and greeting card manufacturers – always send an SAE so you are more likely to receive a reply.

Potential earnings This depends on what the work is used for – a book cover could get you as much as £800, a magazine illustration £300, greeting cards £150.

Tips

- Make sure you retain copyright on all your designs
- When you send in samples of artwork always have your name and address written on it clearly. Accompany it with an SAE for return and covering letter. Follow up about 3-4 weeks later
- Don't send the orginal artwork until you get a contract
- Before you sign a contract check how long they will retain the rights to your work
- Think before you hand over the rights, perhaps the artwork could be used on more than just one card – stationery as well
- Keep a portfolio of your work showing all the different styles you specialise in. It is worth spending time and money on getting the presentation right.

Useful contacts
Association of Illustrators
29 Bedford Square, London WC1B 3EG
Tel: 0171 636 4100

Greeting Card Association
41 Links Drive, Elstree, Herts WD6 3PP
Tel: 0181 236 0024

Morris College of Journalism
The Old School, Princes Road, Weybridge, Surrey KT13 9DA
Tel: 01932 850008

The Registry
'Summer Exhibition'
The Royal Academy of Arts, Piccadilly, London W1V 0DS
Tel: 0171 439 7438

ASTROLOGY

The study of astrology is the study of ourselves and our world. According to The Faculty of Astrological Studies, to study astrology is 'to explore the nature and quality of time… It is the oldest known system for exploring the patterns in our lives and the evolving nature of our world.' With the popularisation of characters like Mystic Meg we are given a misleading view of the value of astrology. There are many branches to it which can involve many years of training.

The term astrology covers areas such as character analysis, predictions, crisis intervention, career counselling, chart analyses for teenagers, children and babies. Growing areas include finance and business astrology. It is a completely fascinating area of study and once you start looking into it, you will find yourself hooked. You could also train to be a Horary Practitioner. This differs from other forms of astrology in that it provides very specific answers to specific questions.

Getting started You need very little, just reference material and charts. Join one of the professional associations who have codes of ethics and offer you more credibility.

Qualifications According to the press officer for the Association of Professional

Astrologers it requires a great deal of book learning and self-discipline. There are about four recognised schools for training, the biggest of which is probably the Faculty of Astrological Studies. This offers a range of courses, day and evening classes, seminars and summer schools, plus a series of correspondence courses. Their diploma course is geared to those wanting to work full time in the astrological field. The course covers forecasting (charts and the history of astrology), relationships (synastry and composite charts); psychology and consultancy (client/astrologer relationships, harmonics etc).

Correspondence courses are useful if you are limited to studying from home – you can start at any time and work at your own speed.

Once you have completed a basic course you could progress to a more specific area such as counselling, taking either a standard counselling course or one specifically for astrologers. Olivia Barclay offers a Horary Diploma Course which lasts about two years and course fees are £350.

Once you have gained your qualifications who must decide in which area you are going to practice. The choices are:

- Face to face basic interpretations of life and character
- Psychological
- Counselling
- Birth charts
- Business
- Forecasting
- Horary
- Medical

Whichever area you go into you will need good skills of interpretation, sensitivity and empathy.

Promoting yourself Advertise yourself through the local or national press. Word of mouth is important and professional bodies have lists of consultants. Target local groups or clubs for talks and demonstrations. One lady astrologer gets most of her clients by talking to people at parties and other social events. Surprisingly men are more interested in astrology than women. It takes time to build up your clientele and is difficult to make a constant living.

Potential earnings This varies greatly. A basic reading takes 1-2 hours and charges start at £50. For birth charts charges are around £65 but it does take half a day to do one before you actually meet with the client to discuss it. For more specialist services you can charge approximately £200. A lot depends on the research you have to do.

Useful contacts

Association of Professional Astrologers
80 High Street, Wargrave, Berkshire RG10 8DE
Tel: 01734 404424

Faculty of Astrological Studies
BM 7470, London WC1N 3XX
Tel: 0171 700 3556

Olivia Barclay Q.H.P.
Mongeham Lodge Cottage, Great Mongeham, Deal, Kent CT14 OHD
Tel: 01304 375667

English Huber School of Astrological Counselling
PO Box 118, Knutsford, Cheshire WA16 8TG
Tel: 01565 651131

BED AND BREAKFAST

If you live in the right area – near the sea, a beauty spot, a tourist attraction or city centre – you can make quite a good living running a bed and breakfast establishment. Generally they are popular with tourists who enjoy the warm family atmosphere they can offer. Your visitors will be looking for home comforts, relaxation, good value and friendliness.

Getting started It won't cost you much to start up if you have a large enough house at the outset. However before you start do your research, check out the competition, are they thriving, what room rates do they charge, is there scope for passing trade and so on.

If you think you will need to modify your property eg put wash basins in the bedrooms, enlarge the kitchen then costs start to escalate. Contact the planning department of your local authority before you start. It's worth contacting the Rural Development Commission (for rural areas only), The Agricultural Development and Advisory Service (if you are a farmer). Local councils, tourist and trade organisations may also be able to offer advice and possibly finance. Your nearest Regional Tourist Board (RTB) will have a list of advisers and consultants. Also useful is an ETB publication, the 'Pink Booklet'.

Apart from obtaining planning permission and Building Regulation consent for property alterations, other legal requirements include:

Fire precautions Under the Fire Precautions Act 1971, you must obtain a fire certificate if you are providing accommodation for more than six persons, including staff but excluding family. Even if you do not need to comply it is good practice to have fire extinguishers and blankets at the ready.

Insurance You must obtain insurance for your guests. If you take in less than six your normal house policy will probably cover your property but you will have to pay an additional premium to cover liability and possessions.

Bookings Once a booking is made, whether verbally or in writing, you must supply the accommodation and similarly your guests must take up and pay for that accommodation. If they don't you are entitled to compensation. Always ask for a deposit – 10-25 per cent is reasonable.

Visitors' register Under the Immigration (Hotel Records) Order 1972, all places where accommodation is provided for payment must keep a record of the full name and nationality of guests. Overseas visitors must give their passport number and details of their next destination. These records must be kept for 12 months and be available for inspection.

Price displays Prices for overnight accommodation must be displayed clearly in a prominent position if you have four or more bedrooms which are not all booked in advance.

Food hygiene and licensing laws If you intend to cater for more than six guests, you will have to register for business rates. Six or fewer, you pay the normal domestic Council Tax, unless the B&B is the main of your home.

Promoting yourself You will need a sign to advertise your service. Local planning authorities have strict guidelines on the size, type and positioning of signs. You are allowed to put up a sign on the wall, or within the grounds, of

---

Bear in mind

- You always need to be on hand if your guests want anything
- Prepare for a certain amount of loss of privacy and intrusion into your family life
- You will have to keep your house clean and tidy all the time
- Increased laundry
- Be prepared to make breakfasts at all hours
- You will need sufficient parking space for guests – this should not encroach on neighbours
- Have a mailing list – your register or visitors book will give you names and addresses. Sending a Christmas card is a nice touch and will remind them where you are.

---

your establishment without planning permission. You will need consent if it is a listed building or in a conservation area or if you want an illuminated sign.

Brochures, however small, are essential. Include details of location, a small map, facilities, prices, information about the area and a colour photo if possible. A word of warning here, remember the Trades Descriptions Act. Don't make your home out to be the Ritz if it has only got two bedrooms. Distribute brochures to newsagents in the vicinity, pubs, garages etc. Local tourist information offices may take a supply. If there is a particular area of interest or sporting event in the locality advertise yourself in the appropriate magazines.

Qualifications You need experience in running a business. There are many training courses covering all aspects of business planning, bookkeeping and even small tourism businesses. Your local Environmental Health Officer can supply details of food preparation and handling.

Potential earnings Room rates will vary depending on your facilities and what the going rate is in the area. Charges can be as low as £10 a night and as high as £40. Your costs will include heating, lighting, food, furnishings, laundry, cleaning equipment, publicity and advertising and maybe additional labour costs.

Useful contacts
Regional Tourist Boards (see local telephone directory)

The Rural Development Commission (see Chapter 8 for address)
The Agricultural Development and Advisory Service

BOOK KEEPING

This is good idea if you are reasonably numerate or have formal training in the
relevant disciplines. It involves keeping track of a company's accounts,
paperwork, bills, receipts, invoices etc. You will have to monitor VAT
requirements and have the books in good order at the end of the year for
inspection by the accountant.

Getting started You will need a PC with accounting software package and a
calculator. Also a quiet place to work and a place to store confidential documents.

Qualifications Courses are available at local Further Education Colleges or
contact the Association of Book keepers. As well as good numeracy you will
need good secretarial skills.

Promoting yourself Target small businesses, go round local trading estates
with leaflets and then follow up with a phone call to the financial department.

Potential earnings Between £10-£15 per hour.

Useful contacts
Association of Book keepers, 44 London Road, Sevenoaks, Kent TN13 1AS
Tel: 01732 458080

CAKE MAKING

Making novelty cakes can be great fun and currently there is quite a big market
as a result of the decline in the popularity of home baking and decrease in home
economics lessons at school.

Getting started A large well equipped kitchen is essential. It will need to
contain a large table top, food mixer and fan oven for batch baking. Like all
forms of catering at home you will have to adhere to the food laws (see page 82,
Catering) and your kitchen must comply to the food hygiene regulations.

Qualifications You do not need any formal training. However you do need to

---

Tips

- Keep an album of colour photographs of your cakes. This is always the best way to impress prospective clients and it helps you to remember all the ideas you've had
- Look for good wholesalers for your staple ingredients like sugar, flour, lining paper, colourings decorations, and so on
- Cook in bulk and weigh everything accurately

---

be artistic and creative, with lots of imagination. Discipline and organisational skills are essential. You must keep to your schedules – a cake not ready on time will lose you a lot of customers. Your local authority may run evening classes in cake decorating although these are less widely available than they used to be. Your local Sugarcraft shop may be able to help and offer advice.

Promoting yourself Advertise yourself through children's playgroups, nurseries, local paper, newsagent, wedding magazines, market stalls – especially Women's Institute markets. You'll find the proof is in the eating. Word of mouth is your best seller.

Potential earnings This depends on your specialism. Novelty cakes are probably the most lucrative area but they are time consuming. When working out your costs time must play an important part. You should be able to charge up to £45 for a large novelty cake.

CAR BOOT SALES AND MARKETS

Selling at car boot sales or from market stalls is an excellent way of finding out if buying and selling really is for you, particularly if you were thinking of venturing into the retail trade. You can keep your initial investments very low.

There is a difference between charity car boot sales and those which are privately run and have almost become markets. Both car booters and the public find that good, well-run charity sales with genuine bargains from people's attics are better than ones where cheap, new goods of dubious origin are on sale.

The car boot sale has changed the face of Britain's markets. Every market used to have its bric-a-brac stall, now car boot sales mean that people can buy second-hand china and glass at prices that are cheaper than market stallholders have to charge.

While the second-hand elements of markets has been lost to the car boot sale, markets are increasingly turning into outlets for individual produce.

Getting started You can sell anything but you must treat it like a professional enterprise even if it is a small car boot sale.

Merchandise should be well presented, nothing should be damaged and it should be realistically priced – for a car boot sale that means quite cheaply priced. Avid sellers tell us prices should always be below £5 and you'll sell most if you stick to below the £1 mark. Don't let this discourage you, every 10 pence adds up.

So what sells well? New shoes, practical kitchen items, furniture provided are complete and unbroken. Steer clear of last year's bestsellers particularly where children's toys are concerned.

Tips

- Ask your town hall about markets. If they say they are full, seek out the market manager and ask if you can come as a casual. Chat to other stallholders to find out any possible ways around the red tape, or if they know any regulars who are planning to leave. Each market is like a community, so it may take time before you feel accepted
- Don't go upmarket dealing in antiques unless you are very knowledgeable in a particular field
- Make sure that you are making a profit at the end of it all, or cost out your time per hour, if you prefer. Don't forget to cost in time spent looking for stock, marking it up and getting it ready for sale
- See how others are pricing their goods
- Don't push or oversell your wares. Sit back and let the customer browse
- You don't need to pay tax if you are selling your own possessions in a car boot fair, but as soon as you buy and sell for profit, you'll need to declare this
- Never forget that you are doing this to earn money. It is all too easy to forget about cash flow and buy things for yourself. Record all transactions in a book and regularly tot up all expenses such as petrol, stall hire, even childcare if necessary.

Qualifications   You will need persistence if you are going to get a stall on a good market, go in with a friend if you can, you will feel less isolated. Choose the right market for your products and you'll find the most individual and unique ones survive the best. Your regular customers will probably be your best ones.

Potential earnings   Aim to take at least £100 a day after you have covered your costs and paid for your stock. Greenwich market in South East London is a haven for craft lovers. It specialises in handmade unusual items from children's joker slippers to candles, pottery, designer clothes, fudge etc. It is this individuality that draws in the crowds every Saturday and Sunday. Handmade items are harder to sell at car boot sales because of the pricing element but your overheads will be lower. The average fee for car boot sellers is between £2.50 and £5, compared with £10-£24 for a market stall. Most people work out the costs of buying or making goods and add a mark-up – at least 100 per cent, particularly on cheap items – or build in an hourly rate.

CATERING/FOOD

This can include making dairy products to sell, baking bread, cakes and biscuits to be sold to shops, hotels and restaurants, supplying ready-made meals to pubs, hotels and restaurants; you can offer a freezer filling service, maybe just for holiday homes, cater for weddings and other events, make jams, chutneys and honey, confectionery; locally made toffees, chocolates or fudge are always popular with tourists and are well received by gift shops.

Getting started   Before you start thinking about a business involving cooking from home consider the following:
- Do you really enjoy cooking? If not, you'll resent the hours spent shopping, chopping and washing up
- Can your kitchen cope? You don't need to invest in a grand kitchen but you will probably need larger pans and dishes and a bigger food processor. Start small and invest in a bigger, better kitchen once you know what you are doing
- Are your premises suitable? They must be easy to clean, well ventilated, properly lit and hygienic
- Don't ignore food-hygiene regulations – they are not complicated and your local environmental health officer (EHO) can supply guidance leaflets.

Alternatively obtain the Department of Health leaflet – A Guide To Food Hazards and Your Business. Local authorities run six-hour basic food-hygiene courses which, although not compulsory, are recommended. You should also register your business with the environmental health officer 28 days before you start if you are going to be cooking for more than five days in any five consecutive weeks. The EHO needs to know you are running a safe, clean operation: they will want to know what foods you are preparing and will pay you a visit to inspect your facilities and operation.

- Decide what you are good at, and make it clear to clients. Specialist cake decorating, for example, is a business in itself, and most home cooks avoid it, but know who to recommend if necessary
- Keep an eye on trade journals for trends, new ideas and legislation, for example, Catering News, Good Food Retailing and The Grocer.
- If you are selling food products remember food composition and quantities must be accurate. You must not make any false claims about price, worth or value. You may be responsible for any illness the product causes
- Follow all food labelling requirements – information packs are available from MAFF Consumer Protection Division.

Qualifications None are strictly necessary but excellent cookery and organisational skills are imperative. Also knowledge of the food laws. Good Housekeeping have a list of cookery schools if you feel you need to improve your skills.

Promoting yourself Think laterally about all the local companies, associations, clubs, groups who may need your services. Target them with leaflets. Consider craft and gift shops, local magazines, wedding events and brochures. Contact marquee hire companies, you could work with them for large events.

Potential earnings To be successful at making money from cooking at home you need to keep tight control on the money and include your time in the charges.

There are different ways of charging, for example per head or for the food and travel costs plus an hourly rate for the time spent. Keep receipts for the food so the client knows where the money is going. Always cost in time spent washing-up, shopping, chopping etc.

Don't undercharge to gain business – the clients will only resent later increases. Write everything down and consider taking a bookkeeping course. If you expand you'll probably need an accountant. At the outset get a deposit from the client before you start on a job to cover your shopping costs, particularly if the order is big.

Doing very small events may seem easier to tackle but you may find you get little profit. For example, if somebody wants a cocktail party at £5 per head it will probably work out better for both you and them if they buy the whole lot ready prepared from Marks & Spencer. Small dinner parties, too, are a lot of work with relatively little profit. Big buffet lunches and events such as weddings are best.

The plus side of cooking from home for women in particular is, of course, that you can have a job without losing sight of the children. However there are times when you will sacrifice homelife because of work. Mothers we've spoken to try to cook when their children are in bed – ultimately you may find you need to pay someone to look after the children.

Food safety The Food Safety Act 1990 was introduced for a number of reasons: the rise in food poisoning, technological changes in industry and the need to implement new EU directives. The Act and regulations that accompany it cover all stages of the food chain from raw material sources to distribution and sale.

Requirements of the Food Safety Act and its regulations

- It is an offence to sell or keep for eventual sale food which is unfit, injurious to health or so contaminated that it would be unreasonable to expect it to be eaten. It also makes it an offence to sell food not of the nature or substance or quality demanded by the purchaser
- Certain obligations and requirements for food handlers, including voluntary workers are laid down
- Food handlers must be supervised and/or trained in food hygiene matters commensurate with their work activity
- All premises used for a food business are required to be registered with the local Environmental Health Department, with one or two exceptions
- Enforcement powers are given to Environmental Health and Trading Standards Officers to enter premises, inspect food, take samples, seize suspect food, prosecute food handlers and serve improvement and emergency prohibition notices. Fines, imprisonment and the closure of businesses are the penalty for breaking the law
- The temperature of certain foods is required to be maintained at 8°C or

below. Hot food must be stored at 63°C or above
- Requirements are laid down for the labelling, marking, presenting or advertising of food and the descriptions which may be applied. Food labelling regulations require compositional standards for certain foods.

Useful Contacts
MAFF Consumer Helpline
Consumer Protection Division
Room 303a, 17 Smith Square, London SW1P 3JR
Tel: 0345 573012

Foodsense
London, SE99 7TT
Tel: 0645 556000

Good Housekeeping Institute (Cookery Schools list)
72 Broadwick Street, London W1V 2BP
Tel: 0171 439 5000

Health Education Authority
Hamilton House, Mabledon Place, London WC1H 9TX
Tel: 0171 383 3833

CHILDMINDING

If you can change a nappy with one hand, model a dinosaur out of plasticine with the other and keep smiling you might have what it takes to be a childminder. Hours of patience, a sense of humour and a sensible but flexible attitude to domestic routine also help. Most of all you must like other people's children. If you don't enjoy being with children, childminding will never be a satisfying way of earning money.

Your family must be supportive – children and partners who resent the invasion of your family life can make things very difficult. Talk to them thoroughly about the implications of become a childminder before you decide.

Geting started The Children Act 1989 requires 'anyone who wants to look after one or more child under eight for reward on domestic premises' to register with their local authority. You have to satisfy them that you are a fit person to look after children and that your home and family circumstances are suitable. Before being registered you will undergo an interview, home inspection, and police checks on you and anyone over 16 in your family.

Some local authorities require applicants who register to take part in a preparation course, which will give you more ideas about how to provide quality care and education. In some areas these are run jointly by the social services and the local childminding association, or by the association on behalf of the local authority.

Registration costs £10; the annual inspection visit costs £7.50. The advantages to registration are:

• Entitlement to apply for public liability insurance
• Entitlement to claim free milk for the children you mind
• Support from other local registered childminders
• Support and information from childminding workers from the local authority which may include toy libraries, equipment loan schemes, drop-in centres, training courses.

The Children Act 1989 also gives social services departments the legal right to make requirements of childminders in their area. Each local authority will have a written policy on its requirements and you can ask to see this. Examples of requirements are:

• Specifying the number of children you are allowed to care for
• That you keep certain records and information about the children you care for
• That you take out public liability insurance
• That you ensure your equipment is safe and well maintained
• That you attend some training sessions
• That you are visited by a fire prevention officer or an environmental health officer, who will also make requirements or suggestions.

If you feel that some of the requirements are unreasonable then you can appeal to the social services department. You must be willing to care for children from all racial backgrounds and meet their needs in terms of language, religion and culture.

After all the checks have been completed and the registration officer is satisfied, a report on your suitability is issued which will include recommendations on approval and conditions of registration. This recommendation will then go forward for approval and shortly afterwards you will receive a certificate setting out any requirements or conditions. It is a good idea to frame this and have it on display where parents can see it. Once registration has been agreed you may start childminding.

It's worth becoming a member of the National Childminding Association which at the start of 1996 had over 50,000 members. It offers not only support but other benefits such as childminding insurance, a local authroity quarterly magazine, and cashbook/registers to enable childminders to keep their financial records in a suitable professional way which is accepted by the Inland Revenue.

Advantages

- You don't need a huge investment in equipment or training – most childminders are simply experienced mothers, or women (male childminders are rare) used to working with children
- Registering is not complicated though it may take several months
- Children can help you with shopping, cooking etc – it will make things more interesting for them if they are involved
- You will become a lifeline to some children
- Contact with other childminders

Disadvantages

- Loss of privacy. Sharing your home with other people can make some families feel invaded
- Dilemma of trying to give your own family enough attention. You may end up feeling torn apart

---

Things to bear in mind

- You will have to make your home and garden completely child-safe – locks on cupboards, doors, gates etc
- You will have to put away all ornaments which children could damage or which could hurt them
- When negotiating your contract with parents discuss any areas of concern such as diet, discipline, TV watching and handling difficult behaviour
- You'll need a contract spelling out hours, rates, holiday and sick pay, overtime, meals provided etc to help in case of disputes.

Number of children Local authority regulations vary but in general the following applies:

- No more than three children under 5 and in some local authority areas only one of these may be under 1
- Up to six children aged 5-7 (if no under 5's are cared for)
- Up to six children under 8, but no more than three of these under 5.

*All the figures are maximums and must include the carer's own children.

You will be inspected annually which is not a test but gives you a chance to discuss any problems and highlight any areas where you would like further training.

Qualifications You don't need any specific qualifications but the National Childminding Association (NCMA) recommends that all childminders should be offered training opportunities throughout their career such as follow-on courses to extend knowledge. Local groups may offer training opportunities themselves. Information briefing and preparation courses are offered by local authorities and give you an insight into what is needed for good quality childminding.

Formal qualifications (NVQs) can be awarded following assessment of a persons competence and ability to perform their work. It is not necessary to attend a particular course in order to prepare for NVQ assessment. You need to register as a candidate at a local assessment centre which has been approved by an NVQ awarding body. Contact NCMA Head Office for further details.

Potential earnings Hourly rates of around £2 per child are average. Good minders can earn up to £30 a day. It is up to you to come to an arrangement with the parents. Most childminders are self-employed and responsible for their own tax and National Insurance. Although income is taxable expenses can take up a large part of any profit and many childminders find themselves below the income threshold for tax and NI.

Think carefully about what you intend to charge: too high and parents won't be able to afford you (check the typical rates with your local authority and ask around locally); too little is a problem, too, childminding is hard work and incurs extra costs. Babies need copious amounts of cleaning up (nappies, wipes, creams etc), toddlers and older children need toys, books, stationery and play equipment as well as regular outings – and all need feeding. Expensive extras like double buggies and high chairs may have to be bought. Electricity and gas bills will rocket and your furniture and decor will suffer, too. And then there is safety equipment such as child-proof locks, fire extinguishers etc which the local authority may insist you have. These, however, are all tax deductible.

Some childminders charge less for two or more children from the same family, but this is up to you.

Public Liability Insurance As a registered childminder you will be able to take out public liability insurance. It is very important that you are insured against accidents to the children in your care and any damage they may do to someone else's property. It can also cover minor claims for lost items etc.

Useful contacts
The National Childminding Association (send a large SAE)
8 Masons Hill, Bromley, Kent BR2 9EY

CHILDREN'S TOYS (See also Crafts)

There is always a big demand for unusual new toys for children – even better if they fit in with the craze of the day, Gladiators or Power Rangers for example. Traditional teddy bears are undergoing a revival at the moment whereas some items such as doll's houses and rocking horses are never out of date and can command a high price. Go round toy shops and chat to the staff to see what sells, talk to parents and children to see if there is a gap in the market.

If you are in the business of board games these need to be more and more sophisticated to compete with computers which are becoming increasingly interactive. If you think you have a good idea you will need to approach the major games manufacturers - remember successes are few and far between.

Safety must be your biggest consideration when making the toys, especially for very young children. Glued-on or embroidered eyes on soft toys for example are safer than buttons. Even special safety eyes and noses need careful fitting.

There are several British Standards which cover toy construction and it is certainly worth getting hold of these if you are going to sell your toys. BS 5665 'Safety of Toys' or EN 71 parts 1-6 which cover mechanical and physical properties, flammability, migration of certain elements, experimental sets for chemistry and related activities, chemical toys other than experimental sets and graphical symbols for age warning labelling.

The Lion Mark is the recognised symbol of safety but can only be used if you are a Member of the British Toy and Hobby Association (to be a member you must have a turnover in excess of £25,000 and all toys must conform to BS5665/EN71).

Getting started You need a good sized workshop. Depending whether the toys are sewing based or involve woodwork you will need all the appropriate equipment, raw materials and tools.

Look out for wholesalers of craft supplies, there are lots around who advertise in the craft related magazines.

Qualifications None are necessary but your practical skills in woodwork or needlework will be important. To invent games you'll need a great deal of imagination, creativity and patience.

Promoting yourself Through nurseries and other child-related groups, the local paper, leaflets, market stalls, car boot sales and mail order. It might be worth thinking about specialist toy fairs, advertising in the trade press or approaching small local toy shops.

Potential earnings This is difficult because it depends on the item you produce. It might be a hand-made dolls house for £100 or a glove puppet at £8. The more unique the higher the price you can charge.

Useful contacts
British Toymakers Guild
124 Walcot Street, Bath, BA1 5BG
Tel: 01225 442440

The British Toy and Hobby Association
80 Camberwell Road, London, SE5 0EG
Tel: 0171 701 7271

COUNSELLING
Counselling is a rapidly expanding profession. If you are seriously considering becoming a counsellor you must first assess yourself honestly and accurately. In order to do this you must be aware of the attitudes of others towards you and discover why it is you need to help others as a counsellor.

According to the British Association for Counselling (BAC), 'counselling occurs when a counsellor sees a client in a private and confidential setting to explore a difficulty the client is having, distress they may be experiencing or perhaps their dissatisfaction with life or loss of a sense of direction and purpose. It is always at the request of the client and no one can properly be sent for counselling'.

Counselling is usually taken up as a second career. If you want to do it professionally it's worth obtaining qualifications and experience in a related discipline such as teaching, careers and advisory work, youth and community work, social work, the church, nursing and medicine. The number of posts in counselling is increasing and they are mainly part-time. However you can set up in private practice and there is no reason why you cannot be located in your own home.

The levels of training of individual counsellors vary tremendously, from lots to virtually none. It's up to you to decide what you need and can offer. Some counsellors build on existing knowledge and work with clients with specific problems, others deal with a wide variety of age ranges and problems. Counselling can be long or short-term: sometimes only one or two sessions, quite frequently 6-10 or even once weekly over several years.

Getting started You will need:
- Knowledge of theory
- Grasp of practical skills (listening, clarifying, helping clients to identify their feelings, ideas and memories). These are best learnt by role playing exercises
- Specific personal qualities, for example empathy so that you can easily put yourself in another person's shoes; acceptance which results from being non-judgmental, caring and supportive; and congruence, the ability to express what you are really thinking and feeling rather than pretending. You can't teach people these skills but they can be developed by skills training.

These skills can best be acquired through training courses, experience in client contact situations, supervision (reviewing what you have covered during client contact with a more experienced practitioner or your peers) and personal therapy (with you as the client).

Qualifications There are no legal minimum qualifications necessary to practise as a counsellor in the UK. However the BAC has codes of ethics and practice to which its members subscribe which aim to promote high standards in both

---

Is counselling for you?

- Get some experience in a voluntary capacity first and take a basic counselling skills course e.g. Samaritans, Cruse, Parent Network etc
- Ask yourself why you want to enter this field – you must want to help others as well as promoting yourself
- Decide what funding you can afford and how much time you have for training. Where can you work to get experience.

---

counselling training and practice. It also has an accreditation scheme which is becoming more important in which you are required to accrue a set number of hours in skills development, in theory and practice. A National Register of Counsellors should be in place by the end of 1996.

If this is a new venture do a short taster course first just to find out if it is for you. There are specialist courses if you wish to go into a specific area such as drugs, alcohol, AIDS, bereavement, cancer, child abuse etc although these are generally for those who have some experience.

The majority of counselling courses are part-time. Some require that you have a degree, other professional training or experience in a related field. Courses range from short counselling courses for those with little or no experience of counselling, up to diploma and master's level degrees. BAC publish a list of recognised courses. There is a courses recognition Scheme set up by the BAC in 1988, courses which are eligible to apply must be one year full time or two to three years part time with around 400 hours contact time.

Workshops and short courses A range are available:
- Introductory courses 6-30 weeks totalling 20-100 hours
- Counselling skills courses 100-250 hours part-time, Aimed at people using counselling skills as part of their job or as a step to full counsellor training. A course of less than 150 hours is not enough to equip you to become a counsellor. Basic courses at an Adult Education Institute 20 hours, costs £50-£60. More advanced training at a private organisation can cost from £500-£1000
- Counsellor training, 250 hours and over. Usually part-time but there are a significant number of one year full-time courses available. Cost, £3-4,000. Add up to £1,000 for supervision. Personal therapy may add on another

£500-£2,000. In total, training to reach BAC accreditation standard will cost around £5-6,000 over three years.

Professional Liability insurance Counsellors are increasingly at risk of accusations of professional negligence. It is worth taking out Professional Liability insurance. The BAC can help with companies who will offer this cover.

Potential earnings A fully qualified and experienced counsellor can charge between £20 and £35 per session. A counsellor in training can charge £10 an hour.

Useful contacts
British Association for Counselling
1 Regent Place, Rugby, Warwickshire, CV21 2PJ

National Council For Voluntary Organisations
Regent's Wharf, 8 All Saint's Street, London N1 9RL
Tel: 0171 713 6161

Cruse Bereavement Care
Cruse House, 126 Sheen Road, Richmond, Surrey TW9 1UR
Tel: 0181 940 4818

Relate
Herbert Gray College, Little Church Street, Rugby CV21 3AP
Tel: 01788 565675

The Samaritans
10 The Grove, Slough, SL1 1QP
Tel: 01753 532713

CRAFTS
This can include anything from making lampshades and drying flowers to furniture painting. The main advantage of making money from your creative hobbies is that it fits in perfectly with bringing up children. You can plan your time around playgroups and school .

Turning a hobby into a career involves very little investment at first, hardly more than the raw materials for a dozen flower arrangements for example or furniture to paint. Start off by selling or giving to friends and family. First commercial ventures need not involve too much capital outlay – the cost of a stall at a charity or car boot sale.

Getting started Choose a craft that you enjoy doing and can work at quite quickly. Carry out initial research into who will want to buy your product and why. Where will they buy it and what will they pay? Remember that gift items must be practical.

You must be able to source raw materials easily.

There may be schemes to assist with funding in your area – try the local reference library and look through one of the guides to current grant and loan support for businesses.

If you live in England it is worth making contact with your Regional Arts Board. If you live in Wales or Scotland contact the relevant arts council – they all have specialist art and craft departments. The type of help available varies but some examples of services on offer are specialised training courses for craftspeople and grant and loan schemes. The Crafts Council offer a setting up Scheme which provides a grant to individuals setting up their first workshop. You can get £2,500 for maintenance and up to £5,000 for equipment. Applicants must apply within two years of starting in business. Those eligible must be working in the field of bookbinding, lettering and calligraphy, ceramics, glass, jewellery, furniture, musical instruments, metalwork, textiles, wood, leather and basketry (painting, printmaking, photography, sculpture, restoration, conservation and reproduction are not eligible occupations). In order to receive a grant your work must show appropriate craft skills and originality; you must have a suitable workshop and a sound business plan.

Approach shops and galleries, visiting them first as a customer to see what sells and who are their customers. Do you like what they do? Send photographs of your work and be prepared for proprietors to implement a 100 per cent mark-up if they take your work. It might be worth talking to people already making the same sort of crafts to get an idea of pricing and pitfalls.

Set yourself realistic deadlines and stick to them. Shops cannot afford to have Christmas decorations in January, or summer stock in late August and people don't like giving late birthday presents, so complete commissions on time. Judging workflow is important – if you take on too much you may not be able to meet deadlines without delegating to other people which is often unsatisfactory.

The Craftsworkers Yearbook lists information on suppliers for many types of crafts. It also has information about craft fairs and guilds and societies. Look out for the specailist craft magazines such as Popular Crafts, Craftsman magazine and Crafts magazine.

Qualifications None are necessary. You just need the relevant skills, flair creativity and imagination.

Know your field and keep track of new fashions. Join local groups, buy magazines and consider extra training. The Crafts Council has a list of short courses, and local education authorities usually run day and evening courses.

Take professional advice if you want to make any significant investment, such as employing people, setting up a workshop or shop, or expanding in any other way.

Promoting yourself The cheapest ways are a local leaflet drop, putting cards in newsagents and advertising in local papers. Send photographs of your work to magazines. Photographs should be 35mm slides, of good quality and adequately represent your work.

There are three types of craft fairs which are worth considering – those held locally in village or school halls, those held more professionally in hotels and halls and those run all year round in shopping centres. Also special events like tattoos and agricultural shows. It is cheaper to exhibit at one of the smaller ones but you may find people are less likely to pay high prices. You'll find fairs advertised in *The Craftsman* directory.

Potential earnings Very little craft products sell at a price that reflects the hours that they take to make. Cost your time out properly, but remember that job satisfaction and convenience are part of the equation.

Keep careful track of all outgoings and claim them against tax – everything from petrol costs to the purchase of a new sewing machine. Keep receipts for all your purchases.

Pricing is variable, for example you can charge about £25 for a child's jumper, much more for an adult fairisle design. The main disadvantage with this type of work is that if it is costed out on an hourly basis, it is unlikely to be very well paid. At first, almost all you earn goes on buying more raw materials or publicising yourself.

Useful contacts
Arts Council of Wales
Holst House, 9 Museum Place, Cardiff CF1 3NX
Tel: 01222 394711

Crafts Council
44a Pentonville Road, Islington, London N1 9BY
Tel: 0171 278 7700

East Midlands Arts
Mountfields House, Epinal Way, Loughborough, Leicestershire LE11 0QE
Tel: 01509 218292

Eastern Arts
Cherry Hinton Hall, Cherry Hinton Road, Cambridge CB1 4DW
Tel: 01223 215355

London Arts Board
Elm House, 133 Long Acre, London WC2E 9AF
Tel: 0171 240 1313

North West Arts
Manchester House, 22 Bridge Street, Manchester M3 3AB
Tel: 0161 834 6644

Northern Arts
10 Osborne Terrace, Jesmond, Newcastle-upon-Tyne NE2 1NZ
Tel: 0191 281 6334

Scottish Arts Council
12 Manor Place, Edinburgh EH3 7DD
Tel: 0131 226 6051

South East Arts
10 Mount Ephraim, Tunbridge Wells TN4 8AS
Tel: 01892 515210

South West Arts
Bradninch Place, Gandy Street, Exeter EX4 3LS
Tel :01392 218188

Southern Arts
13 St Clements Street, Winchester, Hants SO23 9DQ
Tel: 01962 855099

West Midlands Arts
82 Granville Street, Birmingham B1 2LH
Tel: 0121 631 3121

Yorkshire and Humberside Arts
21 Bond Street, Dewsbury WF13 1AX
Tel: 01924 455555

The Craftworkers Yearbook
The Write Angle Press, 44 Kingsway, Stoke-on-Trent, Staffs ST4 1JH

CV WRITING

We all need a curriculum vitae at some time or another. This is the first thing a prospective employer reads about you so it must be a major selling tool.

If you are intending to write someone's CV for them it is important that you have a face-to-face interview to obtain all the necessary details. If they are applying for a specific post make sure you read the advertisement and make use of any details they have obtained about the company. It's up to you to tailor make your client for that job.

Getting started At a pinch you could get away with an electronic typewriter but you will find a personal computer and word processing package much more useful especially as there are likely to be lots of corrections and additions. You will also need a good printer – inkjet or preferably a laser printer.

The accompanying letter is as important as the CV. It must spell out what your client can offer the company and why they will benefit from employing him or her. It's always useful if you can create the impression that you know something about the company and what they do. Encourage your client to do the necessary research. Libraries and career offices will have the appropriate business directories.

Ten golden rules for a perfect CV

1 Keep it short, concise and clear. One page of A4 is sufficient
2 Start with basic details and follow on with experience and achievements
3 Focus on experience relevant to that particular job and company.
4 Highlight achievements and responsibilities
5 Include training and qualifications – you could omit school details and include relevant non-vocational courses instead
6 Leave out leisure interests unless they are relevant
7 Tell them just enough to attract their interest, they can ask more at the interview
8 Use short, punchy sentences
9 Check spelling and grammar
10 Print it on good quality paper, not just photocopier paper.

Qualifications No formal qualifications are necessary, just a good command of English and letter writing skills. It might be worth, as a supplement to your business, to obtain experience or follow a course in careers counselling or interview techniques. It's useful if you have been a manager and carried out selection and interviews because you know what an employer is looking for.

Promoting yourself Consider noticeboards at schools, colleges, adult education institutes, local press, leaflets, trade journals.

Potential earnings The going rate is around £20 for an initial consultation and ten copies of the CV. You can charge around £60 for executive CV's but this is much more competitive and there are many CV consultancies cashing in on this market. It might be worth offering special discounts to students to build up your business.

DESKTOP PUBLISHING

With just a computer, appropriate software and a printer, anyone can become a home-based publisher producing anything from local neighbourhood watch newsletters, brochures, theses, posters and reports to technical drawings and diagrams for magazines.

Getting started The range of DTP systems and equipment is huge and taking expert advice on what to buy and how to use it is vital. Computer magazines are one source, or contact one of the homeworking organisations such as Home Run or Fresh Solutions (see Chapter 8).

A service and maintenance contract may be a good investment, but do check the small print - some companies offer cheap equipment but have expensive service contracts. You may be better off with a simple insurance policy to provide cover for breakdown and replacement. Shop around for the best quote.

Qualifications No formal training is necessary but you need to know your way around a computer and the software you have chosen. There are courses on DTP available at night school or privately run. Look in computer magazines and national press for details.

You need to be able to type accurately and quickly to be profitable and be happy to work under pressure and keep to strict deadlines.

Promoting yourself Distribute leaflets in your local trading estate and follow up with a phone call. Target small businesses which may not have adequate secretarial resources. Advertise on college and university noticeboards.

Potential earnings Variable depending on which area you specialise in.

DIRECT SELLING

According to the Direct Selling Association this is 'a method of marketing consumer goods directly to consumers where sales are achieved as the result of personal contact between a salesperson and the consumer'. Pyramid or network selling is similar (see page 100).

How does it work? The distributor:
- demonstrates the product or leaves a catalogue
- collects the orders
- delivers the goods personally or arranges delivery through the company
- collects payment for the goods or arranges for payment to the company.

The party plan system This is used for relatively low-value products that are easy to demonstrate at parties. Tupperware pioneered this method and it now accounts for 20 per cent of direct sales.

Tips

- Not every one is going to succeed. You need to get sound business advice and have a flair for selling
- Make sure the product appeals to you personally and that it seems fairly priced
- You need a well established social circle to avoid running out of customers
- Don't sit back and wait for the money to appear. Do your research and ensure there is a market close to you that wants your product.

What is network marketing? Independent distributors generate an income by selling direct to consumers and by recruiting them as sellers. The distributor earns commission on his own sales and those of his recruits.

When you progress up the ladder you will still do a little selling and most of your income will come from the sales of your recruits. You will be spending most of your time selling (or presenting) the business plan to others and be responsible for training those people you introduce.

Pyramid selling legislation, included in the 1973 Fair Trading Act, has provided some protection for would-be-distributors involved in direct selling. It's not watertight: a criticism is that advertising and recruitment can be misleading. To be on the safe side join a company which belongs to the Direct Selling Association, a high proportion do. The DSA has a code of practice and a good record for fair trading.

Despite the recession and its slightly tarnished image gained in the seventies, direct selling has increased sales over the past nine years. Consumers in 1994 bought around £948 million worth of cosmetics, household and electrical products, clothes, books, toys and slimming aids through direct sales, 20 per cent through party plan.

Direct selling has a lot to offer the consumer, for example being able to try products at home, taking time to decide and having the goods delivered to your door. Party plan selling is an attractive proposition particularly if you have small children and are tied to the house and enjoy the odd social occasion. A recent Mori poll conducted for the National Consumer Council shows that 40 per cent of shoppers have had enough of unhelpful and uninterested shop staff treating them with 'ignorance and rudeness'.

Getting started Attend a party yourself to see how it operates and if you are interested ask the organiser about opportunities. Contact one of the members of the DSA whose products interest you and you feel you can sell. Some companies will require you to buy a certain level of 'stock/starter pack' or require a joining fee of £25-£70.

Qualifications Research has shown that the best direct sellers are 30-40 years old or retired. To be successful you must be confident, friendly, persistent and often married (so that partners can also become involved), with a fairly established social network. You must be over 18 years of age. All direct selling companies offer training and support.

Promoting yourself Word of mouth is the best medium. If you are just dropping off a catalogue for customers to browse through you will need to target built-up areas to save time and legwork.

Potential earnings More than 90 per cent of direct sellers work less that 30 hours a week and have average sales of £1,400 per year. Only a few full-time direct sellers make millions. It is a good way to earn money if you want to pay off a debt, finance a holiday, or supplement existing income. Typical earnings quoted by companies were: 'Average organisers attend three parties a week (that's about 9 hours work), earning around £40 from each. The hostess gets 10 per cent of the total party sales and a lingerie gift.'*Ann Summers.* 'Organisers earn up to £35-£40 per party, generally attending about two a week. Organisers do not need to buy any stock, all samples are loaned.' *The Dee Group.*

Useful contacts
Direct Selling Association
29 Floral street, London WC2E 9DP

Leading companies are: Amway (01908 363000); Ann Summers (0181 660 0102); Avon Cosmetics (01604 232425); Betterware (0121 693 1000); Cabouchon (0181 213 7100); The Dee Group (01283 566344); Encyclopaedia Britannica (0181 669 4355); Dorling Kindersley Family Library (01403 270274); Herbalife (01753 559955) Kleeneze Homecare (01179 750350); Oriflame (01908 261126); Princess House (01434 606741); The Tupperware Company (01895 826400).

DOG TRAINING

If you feel ready to audition for One Man and his Dog this one could be for you! Dogs are relatively easy to train because they are constantly watching and do mimic behaviour to a certain degree.

Getting started Experience, knowledge and love of dogs is essential. Start by joining a dog training club yourself. Learn as much as you can. Gain more experience through helping out in a vets or kennels.

Qualifications The British Institute of Professional Dog Trainers hold two instructors courses a year and charge £345 for one week (residential). Here you learn to be an instructor. Once qualified you can set yourself up and you don't need a licence.

Promoting yourself Advertise through pet shops, vets and boarding kennels.

Potential earnings On average you can charge about £15 an hour for one-to-one training. You might prefer to do group training sessions and charge less for each dog and owner.

Useful contacts
British Institute of Professional Dog Trainers
Bowstone Gate, Near Disley, Stockport SK12 2AN
Tel: 01663 762772

EDITING AND PROOF-READING

Most freelance editors or proof-readers have started off in journalism or publishing. This is beneficial to build up a network of contacts and a reputation. You can start from scratch.

The best way to learn editing is through hands-on experience under the supervision of a skilled editor or chief sub-editor. That way you learn a house style quickly and know what the editor is looking for. You are checking style and grammar but also for contentious and libellous statements, insensitive stories or inappropriate layouts. For example, it would be inappropriate to have a feature on infertility against an advert for contraception. Good Housekeeping always sends copy to their solicitors if the sub-editors feel it could be a problem. Copy-editors may also have to cut or add copy, think up house style titles and cross heads and write captions.

If you are a proof-reader it can help if you work in a specialist area such as science or technology – your skills are more likely to be in demand.

Getting started You will possibly need a PC and definitely good reference books. It is worth joining a professional body like the society of Freelance Editors and Proof-readers (SFEP) to keep you in touch with what's going on through newsletters, contact with other freelancers and details of meetings and conferences.

Qualifications Full-time, part-time and home-study courses are all available. The SFEP has lists of training courses and runs one-day introductory courses. They are hoping to set up an accreditation scheme for copy-editors and proof-readers. A Chapterhouse one-day proof-reading course costs around £65 and includes style and house style, dealing with publishers, techniques and what the proofing marks mean. Four-day editorial skills courses are residential and cost £450.

You need a good grounding in the English language and excellent spelling and grammar. You must also be able to adapt to differing house styles, be accurate and precise, creative, and be happy to work under pressure.

Promoting yourself Advertise by writing to publishers, specifically the sub-editors who need extra help. It is up to them to get the authorisation. Write a hand-written letter and type out your CV to demonstrate your skills at writing and typing. If you have a specialist area get hold of the Writers' and Artists' Yearbook for details of books and publishers in that area. Contact local publishers or firms who may want extra help.

Potential earnings The average hourly rate for proof-readers is £8.60, £10 for copy-editing.

Useful contacts
Society of Freelance Editors and Proof-readers
38 Rochester Road, London NW1 9JJ
Tel: 0171 813 3113

Book House Training Centre
45 East Hill, London SW18 2QZ
Tel: 0181 874 2718

Chapterhouse Publishing
2 Southernhay West, Exeter EX1 1JG
Tel: 01392 499488

National Union of Journalists
Acorn House, 314-320 Gray's Inn Road, London WC1X 8DP
Tel: 0171 278 7916

FITNESS TRAINER

There are personal training opportunities in all sports – track, field, water or gym. People often prefer one-to-one tuition especially if they have health problems, are overcoming injury or training for a specific goal – a marathon for example.

This is not strictly home-based but the business side can be run from home. You can train clients at fitness centres, in the office or their home, at local swimming pools or by pounding the streets.

Bear in mind that this occupation does differ from working in a gym or a fitness centre where people tend to be under 35 and relatively healthy. A personal trainer will probably be dealing with less fit people, perhaps those with medical problems. You have to be aware of a client's limitations and how to cope with possible problems.

A personal fitness trainer works unsociable hours to fit in with the clients' lifestyle. Your day might start at 5am and finish at 9pm. Burn out is a big problem because of the hard physical exercise, running the business and working long hours. Your own training is likely to suffer, too. At the end of a hard day the last thing you'll want is to do is work out yourself.

Getting started The type of equipment you need will depend on your specialist area. You will probably need transport to carry equipment around.

Promoting yourself Advertising is not particularly successful because the choice of trainer is very personal. Personal recommendation is best. You will have to work very hard at building up your network of clients. Two-thirds of trainers give up once they realise how difficult it is to market themselves. More time is probably spent on gaining clients at the outset than actual training. It is very much a public relations exercise. Give your business cards to friends and relatives; go to fitness conferences, events; leave fliers in libraries, book shops, church halls, gyms and fitness centres.

Tips

- Always make a contract with your client and include in it cancellation procedures, payment details, missed appointments etc. People are notorious for cancelling and changing appointments
- Insist your clients pay for a minimum number of sessions and ensure they pay up front for the whole lot. This will secure your fee and motivate the client
- Get a good insight into a potential client's lifestyle before taking them on. Find out about their medical history, stress factors, diet, habits such as smoking or drugs and exercise pattern. Don't take on someone who is not medically up to it, or at least check with their GP first. Lifestyle screening can take up to an hour, you may wish to charge for the time. Personal fitness training is more competitive and difficult in London.

Qualifications If you are starting from scratch you must follow a course with a reputable company such as the RSA or the YMCA depending in which areas you wish to specialise. There is no one recognised course. Magazines such as *Health and Fitness* list courses at the back. You need to decide your aims and goals, how much time have you got, how much money can you afford on training and what you want to do with the training.

The Association of Personal Fitness Trainers has set up three university diploma courses. Members of the association are graded according to their qualifications. They are trying to set up standards so that the public knows what they should be looking for.

Some training in related disciplines, such as nutrition or stress counselling, will help when promoting yourself.

You need the right personality – you have to be continually on top form. Because you are working on a one-to-one basis you have to give that person 100 per cent or else they will become disillusioned and demotivated. You have to be cheerful, smiling and enthusiastic even at five am on a cold December morning.

Potential earnings The average yearly income in London is probably around £14,000. The highest earner pockets around £40,000 but this includes some income from managing a large fitness centre.

Useful contacts
Association of Personal Fitness Trainers
Suite 2, 8 Bedford Court, Covent Garden, London WC2E 9OU
Tel 0171 836 1102

National Register of Personal Trainers
Thornton House, Thornton Road, London SW19 4NS
Tel: 0181 944 6688

FLOWER ARRANGING

There is a big difference between flower arranging as a hobby and the professional florist. Skills can be learnt and there is no reason why they cannot be carried out from home. It is a very competitive area and therefore important to build up a very loyal client base.

Getting started Tools of the trade include containers, baskets, florist's foam, scissors, knives, ribbons, wrapping, water buckets for conditioning flowers, gift tags and extra accessories for special work such as weddings. You will also need access to a good supply of flowers, probably from a wholesale market, a well lit area in which to work with a bench at the correct height.

Transport is vital for delivering finished arrangements.

A word of warning: visits to wholesale markets will mean early starts. Be prepared for long days to get a big commission ready on time.

Qualifications Although this occupation often begins as a hobby it is worth getting some form of training to at least an intermediate standard. Most agricultural and horticultural colleges offer relevant courses. Trade magazines will also keep you abreast of 'fashions' in flowers and techniques and list private training courses. Some retail experience would be useful.

Promoting yourself Word of mouth will be an important way of building up a reputation. Ask friends to recommend you and send leaflets to businesses. Think of all the occasions people give flowers and target the relevant groups. Consider special arrangements for dinner parties, conferences, anniversaries, Christmas, new babies, weddings etc. Keep a portfolio of photographs of your work to provide clients with a selection.

Potential earnings It depends on the type of flowers and the quantity. Find out what the retailer is charging as customers will expect you to be cheaper. However, this can be difficult because the retailer can buy in bulk more cheaply and has a larger business.

HOST FAMILY TO FOREIGN STUDENTS

If you enjoy the company of others and don't mind intrusions into your family life, opening your doors to foreign students is a good way of earning extra money. Every year about 615,000 students come to the UK to study – many stay with host families. Visits last from one week to a year.

Bear in mind you are taking the students in to be part of your family and so you have some responsibility for their happiness and well-being. Your whole family must be enthusiastic about the arrangements because it affects everyone. Also remember that it is good for children to mix with other races and cultures – it may improve their language skills, too!

Getting started You need a spare room, a comfortable house and an accommodating family. Get in touch with students through your local language school's accommodation officer. The Association of Recognised English Language Services (ARELS) publishes useful leaflets. Your house will be inspected by the school to check that it is clean and has the necessary facilities before you are allocated a student .

Bear in mind the following:

- According to ARELS when you accept a booking it is a legally binding contract. So if the student fails to arrive you are entitled to compensation
- You are going to have to do more household chores
- Increased fuel bills
- You are obliged to make the student one of the family which means taking them on outings
- You must provide a room with bed, desk, chair, bedlinen, heating, drawers and wardrobe
- There should be no more than two students to a room
- You must respect your guest's religious or cultural habits and they should respect yours
- Meals should be taken together. Check whether the students have any dietary restrictions. For example, you may want to specify a preference for a vegetarian if all your family is vegetarian

- If the student disappears without paying contact the school immediately. They may be reported to the Home Office or the appropriate Embassy
- According to the Housing Act 1980 bedrooms in a house of multiple occupation must be 70ft^2 for one adult, 110ft^2 for two
- You can charge the student for damage to your property but not wear and tear.

Tips are similar to those under Bed and Breakfast (see page 76). In addition make an inventory of what is in the room and get the student to sign it and take out an insurance policy to cover the student's belongings, most companies do not charge extra for this.

Promoting yourself Contact the accommodation offices of local universities and colleges.

Qualifications ARELS produce a Homestay Code of Practice for host families.

Potential earnings The going rate for half board varies between £70-£100 per week.

Useful contacts
The Association of Recognised English Language Services (ARELS)
2 Pontypool Place, Valentine Place, London SE1 8QF
Tel: 0171 242 3136

HAIRDRESSING
According to the National Hairdressers' Federation around 50 million people visit a hairdresser in any three-month period. Quite a few of these would rather pay less for the service and avoid the inconvenience of leaving the house.

As a hairdresser you can either work in your own or the clients' home. You will probably have already worked in a salon and decided to branch out on your own.

Getting started? You will need transport, all your own equipment – curlers, scissors, combs, brushes, hairdryer (plus backup in case one breaks down), shampoo and lotions – and your own towels for when you are colouring or perming hair. otherwise you should be able to use the clients'.

Qualifications Unfortunately, the industry is not regulated, so anyone can set themselves up as a hairdresser. To gain the trust and confidence of clients it is advisable to be State Registerd through the Hairdressers' Council. This indicates that you have successfully completed a nationally recognised two-year course or three-year apprenticeship. Once registered you will get a certificate – carry this around with you or have the logo printed on your business cards. The Freelance Hairdressing and Beauty Federation will only accept members if they have a NVQ or City and Guilds qualification and two years salon experience.

You will need to be confident, chatty, cheerful, creative and often a good listener. Keep up to date with new techniques by reading the trade journals and attending workshops and training seminars.

Promoting yourself This is a difficult one because having your hair cut is so personal and important. Most people go with personal recommendations – ask your clients to spread the word. Build up a portfolio of your work – your clients probably won't mind having a picture taken of their finished cut. Try leaflets and local shops. Why not target specialist areas such as old peoples homes.

Potential earnings The most important thing to remember is that you don't necessarily need to under cut the salons. You may not have to pay rent on premises but you will have travelling costs instead. The price you set is really up to you, Some charge as little as £5 for a cut and others £25. Realistically, to build up your clientele you need to keep below £20. Make yourself more attractive by charging family rates or very cheap prices for children. Include a free fringe trim between appointments as an extra.

A big problem will be making money if you have to travel long distances between each appointment. Try and organise your time as effectively as possible making appointments in one area on specific days. However, in practice it won't be so easy as you have to suit your clients.

Indemnity insurance There has been a glut of complaints against hairdressers recently, so make sure you are covered should things go wrong.

Useful contacts
Freelance Hairdressing and Beauty Federation
1 Osmonde Close, Worthing, West Sussex BN14 7QJ
Tel: 01903 234863

National Hairdressers' Federation
11 Goldington Road, Bedford, MK40 3JY
Tel: 01234 360332

Hairdressers Council
12 David House, 45 High Street, South Norwood, London SE25 6HJ
Tel: 0181 771 6205

HERBALISM

A surprising 80 per cent of the world's population relies on herbal medicine for health.

A medical herbalist is trained to diagnose illness in the same manner as a conventional doctor but they also try to find the cause. Once identified they find ways to treat the illness using herbal remedies to restore the body's balance.

During a first consultation the patients total medical history is explored before treatment is given.

Getting started You will need a consulting room with washing facilities, a treatment couch and your own dispensary. Also storage space for the tinctures and herbs.

Qualifications To become a member of the National Institute of Medical Herbalists you will need a recognised qualification from The School of Phytotherapy or Middlesex University.

Promoting yourself
Display leaflets or cards in health food shops, local directories, chemists. Give talks to local groups. Word of mouth, as for most professions, is very important. Professional institutes will maintain lists of consultants. Send an SAE with a 29p stamp to the National Institute of Medical Herbalists for their register of members.

Potential earnings Initial consultations lasting generally one hour cost between £20 and £40 depending on location, Follow up appointments can cost up to half this. Charge for the herbs used – generally around £3-£4– because the cost depends on what your patient needs.

Useful contacts

National Institute of Medical Herbalists
56 Longbrook Street, Exeter EX4 6AH
Tel: 01392 426022

British Herbal Medicine Association
Sun House, Church Street, Stroud, Glos. GL5 1JL
Tel: 01453 751389

The School of Phytotherapy
Bucksteep Manor, Bodle Street Green, Hailsham, East Sussex BN27 4RJ
Tel: 01323 833812/4

Middlesex University, Faculty of Health Studies
Queens Way, Enfield, Middlesex EN3 4SF
Tel: 0181 362 5000

HOME TUITION

A good option if you really enjoy teaching but don't want the pressure of a full-time job or the uncertainty of supply teaching. It is ideal also if you want to work part-time especially if you have to fit in with a young family.

As a home tutor you have a choice of level: you can teach the basics to nine year olds, coach entry into selective schools, help students achieve good grades at GCSE or A level, or concentrate on adults learning for business or just for fun.

For some teachers working for themselves is the only option. Many music teachers for example tend to be self-employed working from home and in schools.

Getting started? Your local Training and Enterprise Council can tell you if grants are available .

Age 3-6: start a small group where children can have fun with music or languages. Established groups include Crechendo (0171 259 2727), Le Club Francais (01962 714036) or La Jolie Ronde (01949 839715) for French – or devise your own. Contact social services to see if you need to comply with The Children Act.

Age 7-10: this is when some children start to fall behind at school, and need one-to-one help with English and maths. If you lack confidence, consider a franchise such as Kumon Educational UK (0181 343 3307). A help package for dyslexic children is published by InTuition (01903 787737).

Age 11-13: coaching for 11-plus and Common Entrance (independent education only) means you need detailed knowledge of the exams set (schools can supply details). Give parents a realistic idea of the child's chances.

Age 16: most teenagers seek help after poor mock-exam results, or for GCSE resits.

Age 18: A-level revision and resits, but also students needing A or B grades for university entrance.

Adults: languages, accountancy, computer skills, craft. sewing, yoga.

All ages: teaching an instrument, singing.

Promoting yourself It is useful to have been in the education system because you will build up your contacts and network. Old colleagues may be able to pass on students who want extra help with their studies.

Advertise on university notice boards, in local papers etc. A word of caution, the advert should be worded very carefully. The first time Jackie advertised in a local newsagents in Highgate village offering French lessons her phone was besieged by male callers. Learning to speak French was the last thing on their mind!

Potential earnings You can charge around £12-£20 an hour for one-to-one tuition. However this intense type teaching does take a lot of preparation so realistically 15 hours a week is the most you can fit in to achieve high standards.

You could consider group teaching. The Kumon works on a franchise system, supplying training, materials and business advice for a fee of £200. Pupils pay £35 a month for twice-weekly classes, plus a £15 registration fee, but you have to pay royalties out of that.

INDEXING

An ideal profession that you can do from home but success tends to depend on who you know rather than what you know. Most indexers have been employed in publishing, libraries, or some other related area and get the majority of their work from old colleagues and contacts. However, if you have qualifications and are fully competent there is no reason why you should not succeed.

Getting started? You don't need much, just slips of coloured coded paper or cards or a computer with a word processor package which will make your job much easier. There are special indexing programs available for the computer when you know how to index – MACREX and CINDEX are the most common. You will also need a good supply of reference books, a dictionary, an atlas and thesaurus etc.

Promoting yourself Write to publishers and authors. Advertise in directories. If you are a member of a professional association they often produce journals or newsletters in which you can advertise. The Society of Indexers, for example, gives lists of indexers to publishers on request. Indexing is used in lots of areas from museums and government departments to businesses and health centres.

According to the Society, if you have a specialist area of knowledge, a scientific background for example, you are more likely to be in demand.

Qualifications There are British and International standards on indexing covering both manual and computer-assisted indexing.

You do not need any formal training but to gain work it is advisable to obtain an indexing qualification. The Society of Indexers offers an open learning course leading to accreditation status. Experienced indexers can become registered after fulfilling the Society's assessment criteria. Other recognised courses include The Book Indexing Postal Tutorials (BIPT).

You must be extremely patient, painstakingly thorough and accurate, have a good level of English grammar, organisational skills, be analytical and logical, command good knowledge of the subject matter and be able to work under pressure to deadlines.

Potential earnings Don't expect much more than £11 an hour. You may prefer to quote for the job as a whole.

Useful contacts

The Society of Indexers
38 Rochester Road, London NW1 9JJ
Tel: 0171 916 7809

The Book Indexing Postals Tutorials (BIPT)
The Lodge
Sidmount Avenue, Moffat
Dumfriesshire DG10 9BS

INTERIOR DESIGN

This can range from small scale room redecorating to barn conversions or complete house renovations.

Getting started Your house will need to look good especially if clients will be visiting you. This is the first impression they have of your work.

Equipment includes a drawing board, a PC with wordprocessing and design software, storage space for reference sample books and so on. Your library area will soon become overrun with fabric books, sample books of flooring, fireplaces, lighting etc. Build up your network of contacts from tradesmen to wholesalers for fabrics, paints and all your supplies. A car is essential.

Qualifications It is useful, but not strictly necessary, to have a background in art and design, architecture or textiles. There are specialist interior design courses although those that are privately run can be expensive. KLC School of Interior Design, for example, runs a 30-week diploma course which costs £11,000 and a 10-week certificate course which costs just over £3,500. They provide good all round training in all the relevant disciplines. Home correspondence courses also available.

You need to be creative, have a good eye for colour, good organisational skills – you may be coordinating several suppliers at once – good contacts in the appropriate trades (plumbers, builders, painters, decorators, architects) as well as a working knowledge of plumbing, drainage, electrics, building skills and regulations, textiles, paint techniques etc.

You will also need a good knowlege of the period house styles particularly if you are renovating old houses.

Promoting yourself Build up a portfolio of your work – include before and after pictures. Place cards in fabric shops, estate agents, paint and furniture shops. Local interior design studios may want extra freelance help – it's worth getting to know them. Distribute leaflets, in suitable areas, printed with pictures of some of your work.

Contact magazines or local papers. They may want to do some editorial on you if you are involved in some successful and interesting projects. Jane Normanton, an ex KLC (see Useful contacts) student, was asked to design Mrs Major's drawing room at the Ideal Home Exhibition. She has not looked back since, having designed look-alikes up and down the country – not a grey one in sight!

Potential earnings This depends on the commission you charge – sums can be quite substantial, especially for complete renovations. As you will be dealing with lots of suppliers and tradesmen encourage them to bill the client direct to avoid committing your own money.

Useful contacts
KCL School of Design
KCL House, Springvale Terrace, London W14 OAE
Tel: 0171 602 8592

LAUNDRY SERVICES

Ask anyone which is their most hated household chore and ten to one ironing will be top of the list. The new man may be around the house somewhere but he is nowhere near the ironing board, according to research by major iron manufacturers. Working women with families and professional couples will be glad to pay to get this weekly chore out of the way.

Getting started Ideally you will want a separate utility room but you can make do with the kitchen. A good quality washing machine is a must, a large semi-professional type would be best. Go for top manufacturers such as Miele, Bosch and AEG. You will also need a tumble dryer to speed up the process – if space is a problem choose a condenser type which can be sited anywhere. Choose an iron with a steam generator, they are more expensive but have a longer lifespan and are more powerful. Find the largest ironing board you can, one with a sleeve board so you can achieve a really professional finish to men's shirts. It's worth taking out extended guarantees for your equipment as they are going to be used continually.

Qualifications None, but it will be hard work, especially ironing.

Promoting yourself Deliver leaflets to houses in your catchment area and advertise in local papers. Word of mouth will become important.

Potential earnings Realistically, the maximum you can charge to wash and iron a large load would be £10-£12. However, if you build up a good network of customers this will soon add up. Offering a collection and delivery service will help build up your client list.

LODGERS

If you have a spare room what could be simpler than earning some spare cash by becoming a landlady. You won't earn a fortune but it can certainly help with the mortgage and bills.

When a marriage breaks down or money is tight, many women make ends meet by letting a room in their house. However, there are several things to bear in mind: lodgers will come and go as they please; they are invading your space, using your electricity and can cause total havoc in the home.

Getting started

- Always take up references from an employer, bank or ex-landlord. (Check them by phone: references are sometimes forged). Ask parents to act as guarantors for students. Get a home address and passport number for foreign students
- Draw up a tenancy agreement, covering the date rent is due, procedures for reviewing rent, deposit arrangements, details of who pays for what, rules regarding guests and use, if any, of the telephone, and notice required. Both of you should sign and keep a copy
- Ask for a deposit (usually between two and four weeks' rent) to offset against damages or unpaid rent
- Give the lodger a record of payments and keep a copy yourself. Sign and date each entry
- Ask for an itemised telephone bill in case of dispute
- Agree to review the situation after two or three months to ensure everyone is happy with the arrangements.

Qualifications None.

Promoting yourself Advertise in local papers, colleges, companies, on hospital notice boards or with personnel departments and at local business centres. Sometimes local Citizens Advice Bureaux have a register of lodgings.

Potential earnings Rents usually range from £25 to £60 a week for a single room, £40 to £80 for a double, depending on where you live. Under the Government's Rent A Room scheme, you can receive gross rent for a furnished room up to £3,250 pa tax-free.

Expenses can be set against tax unless you choose the £3,250 tax-free scheme, so make sure the rent covers heat, light and electricity, and charge separately for the phone, if used. If your income is more than £3,250 you can either:

- pay tax on the excess (after £3,250) without any relief for expenses

or

- calculate the profit from the letting (gross rents less actual expenses) and pay tax on that profit.

Insurance premiums may increase and theft cover might be restricted to burglary only.

You will lose the 25 per cent discount on council tax you receive if you're a single parent or live alone.

Tips

- If you have a mortgage, contact your lender, making it clear you will be sharing, not letting, your home
- Decide which parts of the house they can use. You may want to include them in your family life
- Decide if you are going to provide all meals – if not, are you happy for them to use your kitchen and equipment
- Decide how you are going to split the bills
- State your house rules from the outset
- Think about your family – you will have to split your time between your children and the lodgers
- If you have problems getting rid of a lodger remember you have an unequivocal right to repossession, but you can't simply throw your lodger out. If they refuse to go after reasonable notice, seek legal advice (eg from the Citizens Advice Bureau). In practice, problems are thankfully rare
- Think about providing self-contained accommodation. However, be aware that repossession of self-contained accommodation is more difficult. The advantages are you don't have to provide meals for lodgers or give them the run of your home. In law, repossession is easier when you sublet to someone who shares your bathroom or kitchen.

Useful contacts
Free publications from:
The Department of the Environment
Publications Despatch Centre, Blackhorse Road, London SE99 6TT
Tel: 0181 691 9191

NEEDLEWORK (dressmaking soft-furnishings etc)

The ability to sew opens lots of doors but it is time consuming to make a finished article. Specialise if you can, for example children's clothes, wedding dresses, ball gowns, tailored items, hats, curtains, swags and tails, loose covers, throwovers. Experienced dressmakers recommend you start small with alterations to build up your clientele.

Getting started You need a work room, a large table for cutting out, a sturdy, tailors dummy (useful for fittings) pattern books, an iron and ironing board. Your most important tool is your sewing machine. Don't be tempted to buy a cheap one. One of decent quality will cost around £500 plus extras such as gathering and piping feet, pleating accessories etc. If you want to specialise in babies or children's clothing it might be worth opting for a computerised machine which allows you to sew motifs and a variety of embroidery stitches. Some machines have scanners so that you can create your own designs.

It is useful to have a private changing area with mirror for clients. Invest in some special labels to sew into garments – firms will do any logo for you, Cash and Cash and Able Labels are two.

Tips

- Don't rely on second-hand measurements, always take these yourself. This may involve travelling to people's houses in the case of curtains but it's better to get it right
- Keep abreast of fashion, techniques and colours by subscribing to a good trade magazine such as *Vogue* patterns
- Don't accept commissions if you don't feel the fabric is suitable or hard to work with
- Advise on styles that suit your client otherwise you will be blamed.

Qualifications Needlework skills can be learnt at adult education centres or through correspondence courses. You need experience, to be creative and very good with your hands, a great deal of patience and good eyesight because a lot of close work is involved. Pattern drafting is a useful skill, again there are specialist courses for these. You must listen to what your customer wants and be sure that you can tackle what they are asking for.

Promoting yourself Keep photographs of your work – you can take these yourself during fittings or brides will be often be more than ready to let you have a picture of their big day. Offer a hanging service for curtains as an added extra.

Local papers and magazines and word of mouth are the best media for advertising. Sue, who specialises in weddings, says her 20p advert in a local shop has brought in the most customers. She also suggests diet clubs and contacting private schools, local police force and airlines as an alteration service.

It's worth having good business cards and headed stationery printed – match these up to your sew-in labels.

Potential earnings Mending and repairing items can be quite lucrative if you are a handy sewer, for example: putting in a new zip £5; shortening garments, £3 for a machine hem, £4-£10 for a hand-sewn hem. You will need to undercut local cleaners who offer this type of service. Individual handmade hats can fetch from £50. For curtains you could charge over £200 plus materials depending on the style. For wedding dresses charge about £200-£250 plus material.

For large items you may wish to charge by the hour or by the item – time is your biggest cost. Don't forget to add on time for shopping trips, especially if the customer wants unusual items.

OSTEOPATHY

Osteopathy focuses on the musculo-skeletal system (the bones, joints, muscles, ligaments and connective tissue) and the way in which they inter-relate with the body as a whole. It combines scientific knowledge of anatomy and physiology and clinical methods of investigation. An osteopath uses hands rather than drugs to discover the causes of pain and treatment involves manipulative techniques such as stretching and rhythmically moving joints. After treatment, an osteopath can advise on preventative treatment – for example they can suggest a series of exercises which may help, diet and ways to adjust posture.

Most people consult an osteopath privately although it is becoming increasingly available on the NHS. It can be very labour intensive once you start, hours of 9am–8pm are not uncommon because many people cannot take time off work and will want to visit you in the evenings and on Saturday mornings. It's also quite demanding physically.

A word of warning, you will be alone with patients of the opposite sex in very intimate positions, always be professional and dress sensibly.

Getting started   Setting up a practice doesn't need to be expensive because your most valuable assets are knowledge, diagnostic skills and manual skill in treatment. Relatively little capital outlay is required as equipment is simple and relatively inexpensive. For example you can start out with a simple wooden plinth (one lady we spoke to got her boyfriend to make it for her) and buy more elaborate electric couches as your practice develops. Other things you will need are towels, sheets, pillows, washing facilities and privacy. Equipment, such as a patella hammer, will probably be purchased during your college course.

Qualifications   The Osteopaths Act 1993 has laid down that it is illegal to practice as an osteopath without an approved course of professional education. If you want to study to become an osteopath you will need to qualify at a recognised school such as the British School of Osteopathy. They have a BSc(Hons) Osetopathy course. It is expensive, up to £2,500 in fees. Once the new General Osteopathic Council is up and running then all courses will be standardised. There are also diploma and advanced diploma courses. Training is lengthy and hardwork.

Other neccssary skills include a caring attitude and genuine liking for people, good communication, empathy and understanding as people can be in great pain when they come to see you, a clear and logical approach to problem solving and effective manual skills – co-ordination and finesse.

Promoting yourself   In the past you couldn't advertise yourself but now it is acceptable. Once you build up your client list, word of mouth is your best medium. One lady osteopath started by giving talks to womens groups, at WI meetings and built her reputation that way.

Potential earnings   Osteopaths generally charge £25-30 for an initial consultation with follow up treatments at £20-£25. To begin with it might help to develop your practice by charging reduced rates for OAP's, students, children and those on income support.

Useful contacts

The Osteopathic Information Service
PO Box 2074, Reading, Berkshire RG1 4YR

The Osteopathic Association of Great Britain
206 Chesterton Road, Cambridge CB4 1NE
Tel: 01223 303344

The General Council and Register of Osteopaths
56 London Street, Reading, Berkshire RG1 4SQ
Tel: 01734 576585

OFFICE/SECRETARIAL SERVICES

An ideal occupation if you have good typing skills. You could expand into telephone answering and faxing.

Getting started You will need a PC and printer. Finished work can be sent to a company on disk or via a modem.

Promoting yourself Advertise in local papers, go round your local trading estate and local colleges and put a card in the newsagents window.

Qualifications No formal qualifications are necessary but a good command of English, fast accurate typing skills and knowledge of report and letter formats are all important.

Potential earnings Hourly rates range from £5-£15. charge for postage and stationery costs.

PHOTOGRAPHY

This is a highly competitive area especially if you want to get into advertising, fashion or magazine photography. It might be worth specialising in other areas. If you wish to stay local stick to weddings and portraits.

Getting started Obviously you will need good cameras which are expensive and all the extras such as portable lighting, tripods, lenses and processing equipment, a dark room etc. If you are going to be home-based you will need a good-sized room with excellent lighting to make into a studio. Look in the trade press for second-hand equipment.

Qualifications No formal qualifications are required just determination to succeed and enthusiasm.

For information on photographers, courses and publishers look in *The Creative Handbook*, published by Reed Information Services or Contact published by Elfande.

You can get professional qualifications but most people are self-taught or prefer to work as a photographers assistant to get hands on experience.

Promoting yourself

If this is going to be a serious career it might be worth employing the services of an agent who has contacts in the publishing world. Look at several different agencies to see how they operate – some go out to sell the pictures to the press others keep a library of photographs. You will need to have an extensive portfolio (over 200 pictures) and constantly supply new ones.

If you don't want an agent you will need to advertise yourself locally in newspapers, wedding magazines and local directories. Getting into magazine photography involves traipsing around all the magazine groups and attempting to see the art editor – this can be soul destroying.

Potential earnings If you are at the top of the professional you can almost command your own salary. However, you are most likely to get around £100 an hour for wedding work.

Useful contacts

The Association of Photographers
9-10 Domingo Street, London EC1Y 0TA
Tel: 0171 608 1441

Reed Information Services
Windsor Court, East Grinstead, West Sussex, RH19 1XA

Elfande
39 Bookham Industrial Park, Church Road, Bookham, Surrey KT23 3EU.

PICTURE FRAMING

Good quality and artistic picture framing need not involve great expense and can easily be done at home. There is huge scope for business – photographs, certificates, prints, tapestries, oil colours, cameos, coins etc.

Getting started Specialist framing tools are expensive and will give you a better finish but they are not essential when you start out. All you need is a sharp craft knife, bradawl, ruler, straight-edge pin hammer, mitre block, fine toothed saw, modeller's drill, clamps, vice, staple gun and pliers. Acquire the professional tools when you feel ready to expand.

You will need room for a workshop, a secure area to store the pictures and any expensive tools, a clean area for measuring, trimming and mounting and a 'dirty' area for cutting, sawing, painting staining and gluing. Good lighting is important for colour matching and checking the glass before fitting.

Materials depend on the type of framing you are providing but you will need your basic frame mouldings, mount cards, rolls of brown paper, fixtures and fittings which are readily available from artists' material shops, timber merchants, DIY stores etc. At first don't worry about having lots of glass around your house a local glazier will cut pieces to size.

As you develop your talent venture into decorative frames or mounts – use gold and silver paint, liming techniques etc. Then you can sell just the frames at markets. If you can create something unique and individual the more chance you have of succeeding.

Qualifications This is a skill which can be learnt at home by trial, error and practice. You will need some basic carpentry skills for cutting wood and mitring corners and the ability to select the right frame and mount for a particular picture. Ask the client for details of the room, lighting and positioning so you get an idea of colour and glass type.

If you progress to framing more expensive prints you will need to learn more about 'conservation framing'.

There are many courses available: Lion Picture Framing Supplies in Birmingham, D.J.Simons & Sons Ltd in London and Roy Rowlands, Hedgehog Art and Framing, Bromsgrove all offer training. There is a professional qualification available called the Guild Commended Framer, administered by the Fine Art Trade Guild.

Don't forget you need adequate insurance cover.

Promoting yourself Advertise yourself by displaying cards in stationers windows, photographic shops, art centres and groups, libraries, craft shops, photographers, wedding magazines, play groups. Try and get some free editorial through your local paper. Keep a supply of photos of your finished work and sets of samples – a selection of mitred corners . Market stalls for frames and 3-d ideas, mirrors. You'll be surprised how quickly your friends begin to pick up on your new talents especially around Christmas time.

Join the industry's trade association such as the Fine Art Trade Guild or just subscribe to their magazine, Art Business Today.

Potential earnings Go round a few picture framing shops in your area and find out the going rate. People will only pay what they consider is a fair price. Try and find out if there is something which they don't do particularly well that you could cash in on ie are they slow, do they offer advice, have unusual or just standard frames? You could offer a delivery service as a point of difference. You must supply excellent service, high quality materials, hints on colour and size.

According to Roy Rowlands, a professional framer and member of the Fine Art Trade Guild, there are many different pricing methods, eg double the cost of materials plus overhead allocation and labour cost.

To help with pricing, if you already have a computer there are several programs available – contact the Fine Art Trade Guild for help.

Useful contacts
Roy Rowlands
21 Forest Close, Lickey End, Bromsgrove, Worcestershire B60 1JU
Tel: 01527 876293

The Fine Art Trade Guild
16-18 Empress Place, London SW6 1TT
Tel: 0171 381 6616

Lion Picture Framing Supplies
148 Garrison Street, Heartlands, Birmingham B9 4BN
Tel: 0121 773 1230

POTTERY (See also Craft section)

Pottery making can be fun and exciting and even relaxing. It can start out as a hobby and develop into a money making enterprise.

Getting started You will need a workshop although this can be set up in a relatively small area. Whether it's a cellar, garden shed or garage, you can probably get away with a space about 10 x 10 feet. You will need sink and water storage cupboards and electricity. Plenty of storage space for clay is important which must be kept in cool, frost-free conditions – a garage or in an outside bunker– and buying in bulk will keep your costs down. Think of convenience as it is heavy to lug around.

Also necessary is a claytable for kneading the clay (it must be sturdy, opt for an unglazed wood bench type) clay bins for clay waste, glaze (it needs to be kept dry and labelled) general storage for oxides, tools, kiln furniture etc.

Your biggest outlay will be on a kiln (start off with an electric one because they are cheaper, controllable and efficient). And of course you need a potters wheel. Beginners should look for a wheel with lots of speeds, an adjustable seat, a large easy to clean water tray, a selection of removable wheel-heads and make sure that it is sufficiently powerful.

Qualifications You will need to attend evening classes or specialist residential course. The Crafts Council has details.

Promoting yourself Friends and colleagues will be a good place to start. Try to sell to local gift shops – original locally made items are always in demand. Also investigate mail-order, craft fairs and markets.

Potential earnings Visit local pottery shops and craft markets to get an idea of the going rate.

REFLEXOLOGY

According to the School of Reflexology this is a safe and highly effective way of treating the body without using drugs or surgery. It involves applying pressure to specific points in the feet to create a stimulation through the nerve pathways from the feet to the brain (like acupuncture). By massaging these points the practitioner releases the natural healing powers of the body. During consultation the full medical history of the patient is ascertained.

Getting started You will need a treatment couch (portable ones cost from £250) or mini couch for positioning patients feet at the correct working height, towels, washing facilities, foot lotions etc.

Qualifications The British Complementary Medicure Association (BCMA) qualifying standard is based on nine-month part-time training courses run at weekends or in the evenings with home study included. The course includes training in anatomy, physiology, the theory and history of reflexology and practical application and costs in the region of £1,000. For details of other courses contact the BCMA.

Promoting yourself Advertise in local directories, chemists, health food shops and produce some flyers. Try approaching professional groups offering to do talks and demonstrations. Once qualified it is worth becoming a member of one of the appropriate professional associations as they often have a referral and advisory service to put prospective patients in touch with qualified practitioners. They can also provide medical indemnity insurance through the BCMA scheme. Practitioners may also be placed on the BCMA National Practitioner Register when in membership with one of its affiliated organisations.

Potential earnings You can charge about £15 to £35 for a one hour session.

Useful contacts
British Complementary Medicure Association
39 Prestbury Road, Cheltenham, Gloucestershire GL52 2PT
Tel: 01242 226 70

The British School of Reflexology
The Holistic Healing Centre, 92 Sheering Road, Harlow, Essex CM17 0JW
Tel: 01279 429060

RE-UPHOLSTERY
Getting started It is important to have suitable business premises because this is a very dirty occupation. Dust can reach every area of the home. You need a lot of specialist equipment: a good sized bench (2.5 x 1.2 metres minimum); trestles for support; an industrial sewing machine; shears; staple guns (compressed air are

best); a compressor; a good selection of hand tools, ripping chisels, mallet, tack hammer, knives etc.

Qualifications Training and experience are essential, this is a very skilled occupation. Contact the Association of Master Upholsterers for details of courses. According to the AMU 'unlike working in a factory, you only get one chance to get it right, and mistakes can be very costly.'

You must get experience by working along side an experienced craftsman for several years. Good standards of workmanship are essential.

Promoting yourself Yellow Pages and Thompsons are quite good value as are the classified ad sections of local and national magazines. Word of mouth is the best media.

You might be able to link up with antique dealers who could suggest your services.

Potential earnings This depends on materials used, overheads etc. A three piece suite could cost between £1000-£1500. Like other businesses, don't undersell yourself – the public gets what it pays for.

Useful contacts
The Association of Master Upholsterers
Francis Vaughan House, 102 Commercial Street, Newport, Gwent NP9 1LU
Tel: 01633 215454

Tips

- You will accumulate a lot of rubbish - arrange removal with the local authority (they will probably charge)
- Many of the materials used in old furniture are flammable as are adhesives and other chemicals. There should be good storage facilities
- Insurance must be adequate. However, according to the Association of Master Upholsterers many members have difficulty getting insurance because of the hazards involved and the cost
- Items are generally large so you may cause irritation to neighbours if delivery vans block the road.

SHIATSU

Shiatsu is a Japanese term meaning 'finger pressure'. It relates to a form of healing using the application of pressure to various parts of the body. Similar to acupuncture, it aims to rebalance the body's energy flow. Practitioners use fingers, elbows and even knees and feet to apply pressure to the body's energy lines or meridians. Gentle stretches and rotations of the joints are also applied.

Shiatsu is recognised by the Japanese Government, and increasingly in Europe, as a legitimate form of healing. In Britain it is slowly becoming recognised by the NHS and some GPs will refer their patients to practitioners.

According to the Shiatsu Society it can be used too in the treatment of headaches and migraine, respiratory illnesses including asthma and bronchitis, sinus trouble and catarrh, insomnia, tension, anxiety and depression, fatigue and weakness, digestive disorders and bowel trouble, painful menstruation and some other uro-genital conditions, circulatory problems, rheumatic and arthritic complaints, back trouble, sciatica and conditions following sprains and injuries.

Getting started You will need to be fairly supple as Shiatsu is usually practised at ground level. Necessary attributes include sensitive and nimble fingers, a good understanding of others and yourself, a caring nature and good listening techniques.

Diagnosis is carried out by listening, observing, asking and touching.

Many practitioners work from home because all you really need is a clean, quiet room with natural light and good ventilation. A futon or firm (not springy) foam mattress is essential equipment.

Qualifications No formal qualifications are necessary but you are more likely to build up clientele if you have some recognised relevant training and are a registered member of the Shiatsu Society.

To become a registered teacher or practitioner you must study Shiatsu for at least two years and work with the public under the guidance of a registered practitioner for another two years, during which time you can apply to be assessed by the Society's assessment panel. If you fulfil their criteria you will be a recognised Shiatsu Society Registered Practitioner (MRSS).

Courses include subjects such as anatomy, physiology and pathology. Lists of recognised schools are available from the Shiatsu Society and are offered on a weekend, evening or three-year part-time basis.

Promoting yourself Advertise in local directories, chemists, health food shops and produce some flyers. Try approaching professional groups offering to do talks and demonstrations. Once qualified it is worth becoming a member of one of the appropriate professional associations as they often have referral and advisory service to put prospective patients in touch with qualified practitioners.

Potential earnings Varies according to location: in London expect to charge between £20 and £35 for a one hour session.

Useful contacts
The Shiatsu Society
31 Pullman Lane, Godalming Surrey GU7 2XY
Tel: 01483 860771

TEACHING ENGLISH AS A FOREIGN LANGUAGE (TEFL)

According to the Association of Recognised English Language Services (ARELS), the teaching of English as a Foreign Language (EFL) is worth more than £600 million per year. This takes into account the fees paid by students to schools or colleges, the cost of accommodation and students' expenditure during their stay in this country. Most students come for short stays, around 3-4 weeks in the summer.

Getting started You need very little, just a good supply of original teaching aids and ideas.

Training as an English language teacher has several important advantages if you want to work from home: you don't need previous experience; training is relatively short(the shortest course is four weeks long); you can work full or part-time; and you meet people from different cultural backgrounds. You also get a huge mix of ages from junior level to pensioners.

Qualifications If you wish to pursue a career in teaching English to speakers of other languages (TESOL) having a degree helps but it can be in any discipline. It is more essential that you have a good all round education. Obviously a good command of English is important. Training for the most basic qualification lasts about four weeks and is a very intensive course which covers language analysis, classroom techniques, examination of teaching materials and educational psychology.

Ensure the course you take leads to one of the most widely recognised certificates which are: Royal Society of Arts (RSA), University of Cambridge Local Examinations Syndicate (UCLES), Certificate in Teaching English as a Foreign Language (TEFLA) or a Trinity College Certificate.

It might be worth observing a class or two before committing yourself to an expensive course.

You must be confident and enjoy working with people, have a logical and organised mind and analytical skills. You must have clear diction and enjoy developing new teaching methods to suit the differing abilities. Patience is an essential virtue!

Promoting yourself Contact local language schools, professional associations (see useful contacts) colleges and universities. Try the educational units of various Embassies or local authorities. After gaining experience you may find opportunities in examination marking, oral examining and writing course books and material. If you already have business experience of some kind this type of work may be beneficial for teaching English for Special Purposes (ESP).

Potential earnings Hourly and daily rates vary according to your reputation and clients. Around £8–£20 an hour is usual.

Useful contacts

Association of Recognised English Language Services
2 Pontypool Place, Valentine Place, London SE1 8QF
Tel: 0171 242 3136

The British Council
Medlock Street, Manchester M15 4AA
Tel: 0161 957 7000

University of Cambridge Local Examining Syndicate
1 Hills Road, Cambridge CB1 2EU
Tel: 01223 553311

Trinity College London
16 Park Crescent, London W1N 4AP
Tel: 0171 323 2328

British Association of State Colleges in English Language Teaching
Francis Close Hall, Swindon Road, Cheltenham, Glos GL50 4AZ
Tel: 01242 227099

TELEWORKING

A white paper on Growth Competitiveness and Employment estimates that there were 1.27 million teleworkers in the UK in 1993 (4.6 per cent of the workforce). Research by Mercury revealed that by the end of 1994 pure home-based teleworkers numbered around 1 million.

Teleworkers are based at home and use the phone to contact clients. You are classed as a teleworker if you run a small business from your back bedroom using an answerphone and personal computer. You're even a teleworker if you have a home office, complete with fax machine, photocopier and a modem for sending information directly from your computer to your client or employer. Basically it is not a type of work but a method of working.

You can set up your own telecottage (shared computer resource centre), where you hire out your expensive high-tech equipment, while running your own business or training others. Some teleworkers provide teleconferencing facilities, modems or more simply just workspace and equipment either on a regular basis or for one-off projects. They also offer a secretarial service, word processing and desktop publishing services. There are now around 129 telecottages in Britain and Ireland which offer a huge range of services. Most are in rural areas although some are expanding into towns and cities.

Getting started You need equipment: a phone with call-waiting tone; call diversion (to an answering service); detailed billing; a mobile phone; answerphone; fax, personal computer, laser printer; a modem for receiving or sending electronic mail etc.

Qualifications For training, contact your local further education college, or your local telecottage through the Telework Telecottage and Telecentre Association (TCA). A background in audiotyping, accountancy, computer programming, data input, market research, office services, publishing or translation work can be useful. You may want to advertise, so brush up on your marketing/sales skills.

Promoting yourself Try asking your employer if you can work from home.

The recession has made contract work popular, so if you decide to set up on your own, it's worth identifying the parts of your old job that could be done at home and presenting ideas to your employer.

Contact the TCA who publish several fact sheets including *Commercial Ideas for Telecottages and Teleworkers* and *Getting Started as a Teleworker*. Membership of the Association costs around £24.50 per annum and entitles you to a copy of Teleworker magazine six times a year. The Association forms a sort of support network for its members – after all working alone can be disheartening and lonely.

You could also contact the National Association of Teleworkers (NAT). Membership is open to individuals and companies using teleworkers. Subscription costs approximately £47.00 which gets you a quarterly newsletter, Teleworking UK and European Journal of Teleworking; use of the NAT code of conduct; access to a database of members who wish to have the details of their teleworking business made available to potential customers; access to the NAT quality assurance system known as Quality Management for Teleworking; the opportunity to join special interest groups aimed at discussing and developing relevant issues; training courses for first time teleworkers and their managers. They also have numerous fact sheets on commercial ideas for teleworkers and finding work.

Potential earnings Variable. Depends on choice of occupation.

Useful contacts
The TCA
WREN Telecottage, Stoneleigh Park, Kenilworth, Warwickshire CV8 2RR
Tel: 0800 616008

National Association of Teleworking
The Island House, Midsomer Norton, Bath, Avon BA3 2HL
Tel: 01761 413869/01761 413869 (membership enquiries)

TELESALES
This involves cold-calling people and trying to sell products, from double glazing to water filters and fitted kitchens. Be prepared for abuse and rudeness from those you call. Remember they have not asked you to and it can be intrusive.

Potential earnings   Variable: go for a deal which gives you a basic salary – commission only may seem more lucrative but wait and see how you get on first. Make sure the company pays for all the phone calls you make. Look in the newspaper for ads.

TOURISM AND LEISURE

Activities could include running a guest house or small hotel; providing bed and breakfast accommodation; running a camping site; hiring boats; tea-rooms; guided tours and walks; souvenir and gift shops; open farms; craft centres; formal gardens or nursery; pony trekking; special interest days or events such as bird watching, art and photography.

Getting started   This clearly depends on you having the facilities for your chosen activity, and some interest or experience in it. Contact the relevant association for advice on how to set yourself up.

Qualifications   Depends on the activity. Anyone can give a guided tour but you would need some experience with horses to run pony trekking excursions.

Promoting yourself   The English Tourist Board and Regional Tourist Boards help to promote and develop tourism in England. They give practical advice on how to set up and run a tourism project, and can help with marketing by mentioning your enterprise in their official guides and publications. The Sports Council can make grants and loans available for sporting and recreational projects. The Countryside Commission offers grants and advice on informal recreational projects. English Heritage can offer grants to farmers for the survey of historic features on their land, with a view to setting up farm trails, and for the provision of educational facilities.

Useful contacts

Association of British Riding Schools
Queens Chambers, 38-40 Queens Street, Penzance, Cornwall TR18 4BN
Tel 01736 69440

Countryside Commission
John Dower House, Crescent Place, Cheltenham, Glos. GL50 3RA
Tel: 01242 521381

English Heritage
Fortress House, 23 Saville Row, London W1X 1AB
Tel: 0171 973 3000

English Tourist Board
Thames Tower, Black's Road, London W6 9EL
Tel: 0181 846 9000

Scottish Tourist Board
23 Ravelston Terrace, Edinburgh EH4 3EU
Tel: 0131 332 2433

The Sports Council
16 Upper Woburn Place, London WC1H 0QP
Tel: 0171 388 1277

Scottish Sports Council
Caledonia House, South Gyle, Edinburgh EH12 9DQ
Tel: 0131 317 7200

Sports Council for Wales
National Sports Centre for Wales, Sophia Gardens, Cardiff CF1 9SW
Tel: 01222 397571

TRANSLATING

Translating and interpreting are very skilled jobs, easily done at home if you have
the necessary qualifications. The emergence of the EU means there is now more
opportunity for translation work particularly if you can specialise in a certain area
such as technology or marketing. A translator has to be able to understand text
written in one language and convert it into a text that has the same meaning,
style and associations to a reader of another language. According to the Institute
of Translation and Interpreting to make a reasonable income you must have a
combination of languages and subject knowledge.

Getting started A wordprocessor and a good quality printer, such as a laser
printer, a fax machine and specialised reference material including dictionaries
are all essential. Indemnity insurance is advisable.

Qualifications Formal qualifications are a must. A modern language degree and a postgraduate diploma qualification are recommended. The Institute of Translating and and Interpreting (ITI) and Institute of Linguists (IOL) offer information on undergraduate, postgraduate and correspondence courses in the UK. The (IOL) offers a Diploma in Translation (DipTrans IOL) in over 40 languages. You will need to gain experience but like many occupations it is a chicken and egg situation – you need experience to get an assignment, so how do you get the experience.

You may also need knowledge of a specific subject area in business or industrial fields. Trustworthiness is important because you will be dealing with a lot of confidential material.

Keep up to date with your language by subscribing to the appropriate trade magazines. The IOL provides a Translators Pack and advice for newcomers.

Promoting yourself Many freelance translators tend to work for translation agencies (contact the IOL) and companies (contact them direct). Send them your CV and a covering letter. You may then be asked to submit samples of your work or they may give you a test piece.

Join an appropriate professional body who will list qualified members and organise workshops and conferences where you can network. The ITI has a 'guardian angel' scheme whereby it puts new translators in touch with established ones. They can offer lots of advice on presentation, reference sources and standards. Quality papers and trade journals will also advertise jobs.

If you want to specialise in books try the *Writers' and Artists' Yearbook* which includes a list of publishers and general advice for translators. The Society of Authors publish a *Quick Guide to Literary Translation* priced at £1.00.

Potential earnings It varies according to the language. Translating English into a European language, £56–£65; English into Chinese £150 per thousand words. Rates are slightly lower for converting a foreign language into English. Book work may be costed out per assignment - think carefully first about the length of time involved. Interpreters can charge around £25 an hour.

Useful contacts

Institute of Linguists
24a Highbury Grove, London N5 2DQ
Tel: 0171 359 7445

Translators' Association
Society of Authors, 84 Drayton Gardens, London SW10 9SB
Tel: 0181 373 6642

Institute of Translation and Interpreting
377 City Road, London EC1V INA
Tel: 0171 713 7600

WRITING

Well they say there is a novel in all of us and if you believe all the ads it sounds easy. In reality, of course, the story is very different. Writing is a very competitive business. There are over 7,000 publications in this country all needing good stories. In addition UK publishers publish around 35,000 new titles per year.

There are many different fields from writing children's stories and magazine features to hard hitting news stories. You could always consider writing for radio or TV. Scripts should be sent to the British Broadcasting company or producers and commissioning editors of the independent television companies. A free leaflet on writing radio plays is available from the Literary Manager (Radio Drama) at the BBC.

If you aim to go into newspapers they want originality not necessarily personal opinion – make yourself the expert. If you want to start a new column you will need lots of fresh ideas. Interviews with celebrities are popular but make sure you find the right audience.

If you want to write for magazines start at the lower end to develop your skills where it is less competitive. Write about subjects you are familiar with and interested in.

Getting started You need ideas and more ideas and a word processor. Presentation is important: it should be in unjustified type, double spaced on A4 paper. The pages should be numbered with a word count at the beginning.

Qualifications There are many courses available - contact the Institute of Journalists for details. You will need a good knowledge of English, creativity, flair, imagination, have an endless supply of ideas, enthusiasm and determination. The ability to work under pressure to meet deadlines is also essential.

Promoting yourself If you are targeting magazines or newspapers find out the name of the commissioning editor or the head of the department relevant to your specialism. Send in a list of your ideas and an outline sketch of what you plan to write and follow up with a phone call about a week later. You will need to study the publication carefully to ensure you have the right angle and house style. There is no point wasting your own and the editor's time by sending articles on the home to a hard-hitting features magazine. Try and get hold of their reader profile and circulation.

It's worth obtaining a copy of the Writers' and Artists' Yearbook which lists all the relevant publications, publishers and societies.

Once you have clinched a deal and agreed your fee write a letter confirming what you have agreed – word count, topic, art work, publication date and so on. This is your contract, editors never send out formal contracts so this is your proof of agreement.

Potential earnings Features can be anything from £50 per thousand words. Books from a few hundred pounds to hundreds of thousands of pounds.

Useful contacts
BBC Drama Group
BBC Television Centre, Wood Lane, London W12 7RJ
Tel: 0181 743 8000

BBC Radio Drama
Broadcasting House, Portland Place, London W1A 1AA

The Institute of Journalists
2 Dock Offices, Surrey Quays Road, London SE16 2XU
Tel: 0171 252 1187

The Society of Authors
84 Drayton Gardens, London SW10 9SB
Tel: 0171 73 6642

Writers' and Artists' Yearbook
A & C Black (Publishers) Limited, 35 Bedford Row, London WC1R 4JH
Tel: 0171 242 0946

USEFUL ADDRESSES

Chapter 1
Home Run magazine
Active Information
Cribau Mill
Llanvair Discoed
Chepstow NP6 6RD
Tel: 01291 641222

Chapter 2
British Venture Capital Association
Essex House
12-13 Essex Street
London WC2R 3AA
Tel: 0171 240 3846

Department for Trade and Industry
(no central address – call the number
below for local address to contact)
Tel: 0171 215 5000

Development Board for Rural Wales
Ladywell House
Newtown
Powys SY16 1JB
Tel: 01686 626965

Highlands and Islands Development
Board
Bridge House
20 Bridge Street
Inverness IV1 1QR
Tel: 01463 234171

Livewire
Hawthorn House
Forth Banks
Newcastle-upon-Tyne NE1 3SG
Tel: 0191 261 5584

Local Enterprise Development Unit
(LEDU)
LEDU House
Galwally BT8 4TB
Tel: 01232 491031

The Princes Youth Business Trust
18 Park Square East
London NW1 4LH
Tel: 0171 543 1234

The Rural Development Commission
141 Castle Street
Salisbury
Wiltshire SP1 3TP
Tel: 01722 336255

Scottish Development Agency
120 Bothwell Street
Glasgow G2 7JP
Tel: 0141 248 2700

Welsh Development Agency
Principality House
The Friary
Cardiff CS1 4AE
Tel: 0345 775577

Chapter 3
British Franchise Association
Thames View
Newtown Road
Henley-on-Thames
Oxon RG9 1HG
Tel: 01491 578050

Chartered Institute of Patent Agents
Staple Inn Buildings
High Holborn
London WC1V 7PZ
Tel: 0171 405 9450

Data Protection Department 1
Wycliffe House
Water Lane
Wilmslow
Cheshire SK9 5AX
Tel: 01625 545745
Fax: 01625 524510

Home Office Insurance Companies
Tolson Messenger
148 King Street
London W6 0QU
Tel: 0181 741 8361

ITT London and Edinburgh
The Warren,
Warren Road
Worthing
West Sussex BN14 4OD
Tel: 01903 820820

Michael Pavey Insurance Brokers
Berwyn House
70–72 Abbey Road
Torquay TQ2 5NH
Tel: 01803 211236

NACCOS
Queensgate House
14 Cookham Road
Maidenhead
Berks SL6 8AJ
Tel: 01628 37512

The Patent Office
25 Southampton Buildings
London WC2A 1AY
Tel: 0171 438 4778

S-Tech Insurance Services Ltd
154–156 Victoria Road
Cambridge CB4 3DZ
Tel: 01223 324233

Chapter 4
UK Newsletter Association
Queens House
28 Kings Way
London WC2B 6JR
Tel: 0171 379 6268

Chapter 5
Homelodge Buildings Ltd
Kingswell Point
Crawley
Winchester SO21 2PU
Tel: 01962 881480

INDEX